Illustrated Māori PLACE NAMES

Illustrated Māori
PLACE NAMES

A.W. Reed

REED

Photo credits

Front cover: Top from left to right; Holger Leue, Holger Leue, Stephen Robinson. Centre left and right; Holger Leue. Bottom from left to right; Stephen Robinson, Stephen Robinson, Holger Leue.

Back cover: Top from left to right; Stephen Robinson, Holger Leue, Stephen Robinson. Bottom from left to right; Holger Leue.

Inside pages: Martin Barriball: pages 19, 62, 83

Nic Bishop: pages 26, 72 (right), 91

Peter Janssen: page 90

Holger Leue: pages 3 (top), 5, 7 (top and bottom right), 8, 10 (top), 12, 13 (right), 17, 18, 21, 23, 24, 25, 27, 28 (right), 31 (left), 32, 33 (left), 35, 37, 42 (left), 44, 46, 50 (right), 52, 53 (top and bottom), 55 (left), 56, 57, 58 (left), 64, 65 (right), 70, 75, 77, 78, 80 (top), 81 (right), 84 (left), 85, 86 (left), 87, 96 (left and right), 99 (left), 101

Bob McCree: pages 3 (bottom right), 22, 29, 30, 31 (right), 33 (right), 42 (right), 43, 49, 55 (right), 58 (right), 61, 81 (left), 84 (right), 86 (right), 94 (left), 97, 98 (right)

Stephen Robinson: pages 3 (bottom left), 7 (bottom left), 9, 10 (bottom left and right), 11, 13 (left), 14, 20 (left and right), 28 (left), 38, 45, 48, 50 (left), 51, 54, 60, 63, 65 (left), 67, 68, 71, 72 (left), 73, 80 (bottom), 88, 89, 93, 94 (right), 95 (left and right), 98 (left), 99 (right), 100

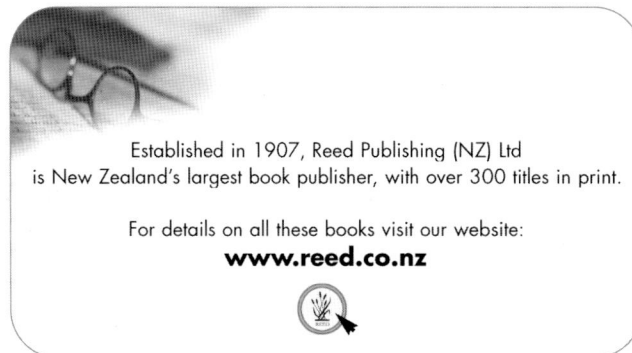

Established in 1907, Reed Publishing (NZ) Ltd
is New Zealand's largest book publisher, with over 300 titles in print.

For details on all these books visit our website:
www.reed.co.nz

Published by Reed Books, a division of Reed Publishing (NZ) Ltd,
39 Rawene Road, Birkenhead, Auckland.
Associated companies, branches and representatives throughout the world.

ISBN 0 7900 0794 0

© Literary Productions Ltd

First published in 1961 as *A Dictionary of Maori Place Names*
This edition 2001

Designed by Nicole Merrie

Printed in China

Foreword

This book is the successor to *Maori Place Names and their Meanings*, which was first published in 1950 and which has been reprinted a number of times. It is now felt that the time has come when it should be completely revised, and enlarged by the inclusion of more factual material than the earlier book was able to provide.

A personal word of explanation may not be out of place. *Maori Place Names and their Meanings* was compiled by the present author because of the need that had been expressed for a book of this kind. Information was sought from obvious sources such as the *New Zealand Official Year Book* for 1919, in which the late Elsdon Best had given a brief list of meanings of Māori names; Mr Johannes C. Andersen's *Māori Place Names*; Mr G.G.M. Mitchell's *Māori Place Names of Buller County*, and other works which were readily accessible.

It was realised at the time that there are many problems to be faced in attempting a literal translation of Māori place names, many of which go back to early days; some indeed were used in the homeland of Hawaiki and transplanted to the soil of Aotearoa (New Zealand). Others had their origins in history and legend and have been lost, or are too long to recount in a small book. Some

names have suffered alteration and distortion; some are modern names; some are too easily translated, giving false and ludicrous conclusions; and some are quite untranslatable.

On the other hand the Māori was closer to nature than the Pākehā (white man); common words for wood and water, wind and cloud and soil were frequently incorporated in his names. Commonsense and direct translation provided most of the answers in the original collection, although it was always acknowledged that a more comprehensive and documented work would eventually be required.

As it happened, the task of putting together the first reference book was the start of a fascinating hobby, which has resulted in a collection of the origins of place names in New Zealand. The fruits of some of this work will be found in the present book.

The information contained in *Māori Place Names* has been gathered from hundreds of books, and through correspondence and conversation with many who are able to provide specialised knowledge in different parts of the country.

Some of the limitations of the first collection still apply, for a really satisfactory answer can seldom be supplied to the question 'What does this name mean?' The Pākehā reader will realise how futile it would be to attempt to translate English names in New Zealand for the benefit of Māori readers; what would he make, for instance, of such names as Gore, Nightcaps, Huntly, Cashmere, Fortrose, Dunedin, Auckland, Shotover and Drury? A similar problem faces us when we attempt to make a literal translation of Māori names.

On the other hand, sufficient historical and legendary tradition has been preserved to enable us to say with some certainty how some names were determined, and to give their meanings. We trust that the interested reader may find interesting glimpses of Māori life in the short notes which are attached to some of the names.

In order to assist the reader, the names have been broken up into their several components, with a translation of the words which these comprise. If sense can be made of the resulting words, a meaning has been attempted. But it must be emphasised that this meaning is no more than an attempt at translating a word, a phrase or a sentence from one language to another. The interested reader who is equipped with a Māori dictionary may himself arrive at an equally satisfying translation.

A comprehensive selection of names has been made, but a large volume would be required to include every Māori place. All the best-known and more important Māori names are included, but there is also a selection of older names which are no longer in use but which most readers may come across at some time or another — an obvious

example is Aorangi, the Māori name for Mount Cook. Some lesser-known names are mentioned because of the interest attached to their origin.

The appendix consists of Pākehā names to which reference is made in the test. These may be Pākehā names which have replaced the original Māori name, or they may list Māori place names in towns and cities; e.g., under Wellington will be found references to the suburbs of Hataitai and Rongotai, which are listed in the main part of the book.

Some thought has been spent on the question of giving an indication of the location of the various places, but it is felt that this is outside the scope of the present book. Such a gazetteer would suffer through the absence of Pākehā names and by the frequent duplication of Māori names, e.g., Wairoa, found again and again in various parts of New Zealand.

It is hoped that this excursion into the meanings of Māori place names will prove stimulating to the reader, who may well be encouraged to make his own investigations. To assist those who are interested, or who may require the meaning of a name of some place not included in this book, a list of words which commonly form a part of Māori place names will be found at the beginning of the book. Readers who wish to extend their interest in the subject are recommended to the *Reed Concise Māori Dictionary*; those whose studies carry them further would be well advised to seek *The Reed Dictionary of Modern Māori*.

A.W. Reed

Hints on pronunciation

There are only fifteen letters in the Māori alphabet:

A E H I K M N O P R T U W NG and WH.

Every syllable in Māori ends in a vowel, which makes the proportion of vowels to consonants much higher than in English. The vowel sounds are therefore of great importance. While the quantity of each of these vowels may vary, and thus change the meaning of a word, such differences are beyond the capacity of the average Pākehā. The following list should be learned by heart:

A is always pronounced as the a in 'rather'.
E is always pronounced as the e in 'ten'.
I is always pronounced like the ee in 'seen'.
O is always pronounced like the o in 'border'.
U is always pronounced like the oo in 'bloom'.

When two vowels come together each is given its proper sound.

The compound consonants *ng* and *wh* are the two stumbling blocks in the way of correct pronunciation. The sound *ng* is that of the middle *ng* in the word 'singing'. Note that in the South Island the *ng* is usually replaced by *k*; for example, Aorangi becomes Aoraki.

Wh is usually pronounced as *f*. This is not the correct sound, which has been described as *f* but without letting the top teeth touch the lower lip. If you cannot manage this, the sound of *f* will pass muster.

These are simple rules, but if they are mastered you will never again be guilty of referring to Te Awamutu as 'Tee-Amoot', or to Wanganui as 'Wangganuee'.

Words which commonly form part of Māori place names

Ahi fire.
Ao cloud.
Ara path or road.
Ata shadow.
Atua god.
Awa river, channel, gully or valley.
Haka dance.
Hau wind.
Hua fruit, egg.
Ika fish.
Iti small.
Kai food, or eat.
Kino bad.
Mā white or clear.
Mā (short for *manga*)
Manga branch, tributary or stream.
Manu bird.
Mata headland, point, surface, eye, raw.
Matā flint, quartz or obsidian.
Mātā heap, plant.
Maunga mountain.
Moana sea.
Motu island.
Muri end.
Mutu end, finished.
Nui big, or plenty of.

O of.
Ō the place of.
One mud, sand or beach.
Pā fortified village.
Pae ridge, or resting place.
Papa broad, flat, or ground covered with vegetation.
Pō night.
Puke hill.
Puna spring of water.
Rangi sky.
Rau hundred, many or leaf.
Riki small or few.
Roa long or high.
Roto lake.
Rua cave, hollow or two.
Tahi one, single.
Tai sea, coast or tide.
Tapu forbidden or sacred.
Tea white or clear.
Wai water.
Waka canoe.
Whanga bay, inlet, or stretch of water.
Whare house.
Whata raised platform for storing food.
Whenua land or country.

A

Ahaura Probably a corrupt form of Ō-hauroa. Ō (the place of); *hauroa* (height). As the township of Ahaura is on an elevation, and the local Māori say that the name means a cliff, the meaning is doubtless The place of a cliff.

Ahiaruhe *ahi* (fire); *aruhe* (fern-root). Fire for roasting fern-root. Fern-root was an important food for the Māori. It was roasted over a fire and pounded with wooden beaters.

Ahikiwi *ahi* (fire); *kiwi* (native flightless bird). Fire on which kiwi were cooked.

Ahimanawa *ahi* (fire); *manawa* (heart). A chief named Tarewa-a-rua was slain by his enemies. His heart was torn out, cooked, and eaten. The Ahimanawa Range has a similar origin. To avenge himself for the death of his daughter, the chief Te Kohipipi surprised his enemies by night. In the early morning he cut out the hearts of those he had killed. He put them in a flax kit and took them home. Half-way up the range he rested, lit a fire and ate some of the hearts. The range was then known as Te Ahi-manawa-a-Te-Kohipipi (The fire of the hearts of Te Kohipipi).

Ahipara *ahi* (fire); *para* (various roots used for food). Fire for roasting fern-root, a staple of the traditional Māori diet.

Ahipara Bay.

Ahitarakihi *ahi* (fire); *tarakihi* (an edible fish). Fire at which the tarakihi was roasted

Ahitītī *ahi* (fire); *tītī* (mutton-bird). Fire for cooking mutton-birds.

Ahuahu To heap up. This is the Māori name for Great Mercury Island. Paikea came to this island on the back of a whale. He was cold and heaped the warm sand over him, and from this event he gave the island its name.

Ahuriri Named after Tu Ahuriri, who found the lagoon blocked so that the flood destroyed the shellfish. He organised a working party to clear a channel to the sea, and the area was named after him. The missionary William Colenso, however, said that the name means 'fierce rushing', an allusion to the swift current in the channel where the river runs into the sea.

Ahuroa *ahu* (heap or mound); *roa* (long).

Akaaka Fibrous roots.

Ākarana The Māori form of Auckland.

The gateway to Aotea Square, Auckland.

Akaroa *aka* (South Island form of *whanga*: harbour); *roa* (long). Long harbour.

Whalers' pots, Akaroa Harbour.

Akatārawa The original form of the name may have been Akatarewa. *Aka* (vine); *tārewa* (trailing). Trailing vines.

Akatore The correct form is Akatorea. *Aka* (South Island form of *whanga*: harbour); *tōrea* (wading bird). Torea harbour.

Akeake A native tree.

Akerama This is the Māori form of the name Aceldama, 'field of blood', the name given at the time the first missionaries came to North Auckland.

Ākitio *aki* (to smash); *tio* (piercing cold). It is said that the name came from a famous greenstone mere (club).

Amokura The name of a tropical bird which visits New Zealand. It is distinguished by two brilliant red tail-feathers. The name was given in 1929.

Amuri Correctly, Haumuri, which means an east wind, or 'the wind at your back'.

Anakiwa *ana* (cave); *a* (of); *Kiwa* (a man's name). Kiwa was also one of the gods of the ocean. The cave of Kiwa.

Anatoki *ana* (cave); *toki* (adze). Cave of the adze.

Anaura This may be a name which has come from Mangaia in the Cook Islands. In a true Māori form it would be Anakura. *Ana* (cave); *kura* (red). Red cave.

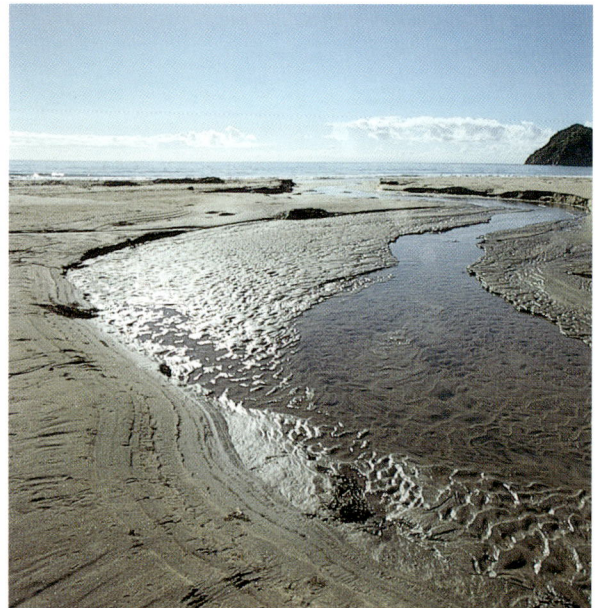
Anaura Bay.

Anawhakairo *ana* (cave); *whakairo* (to paint or carve in a pattern). In this cave on the banks of the Waitaki River near Coal Creek, the water has carved out recesses in the rock wall, and there are fantastically shaped pinnacles and round, window-like holes. Cave of carved or sculptured rock.

Anawhata *ana* (cave); *whata* (food-store). Cave of the food-store.

Āniwaniwa Rainbow.

Aohanga A variety of flax. The name has appeared at various times as Ohonga, Ohanga, and Aohanga, but the correct form is probably Ōwahanga. *Ō* (the place of); *wahanga* (mouths). The name was applied to the river as a whole.

Aokaparangi *ao* (cloud); *kapa* (row or rank); *rangi* (sky). A row of clouds in the sky.

Aokautere *ao* (cloud); *kautere* (to float or move swiftly). Swiftly moving clouds.

Aongatete *ao* (cloud); *ngatete* (to move). Moving clouds.

Aorangi *ao* (cloud); *rangi* (sky). Cloud in the sky. This is one of the Māori names for Mount Cook, the highest mountain peak in the country. The other is Kirikiri-Katata. Aorangi is popularly translated as Sky-piercer, but this is incorrect. The South Island Māori called it Aoraki, because *raki* is the South Island pronunciation of *rangi*. There are several explanations of the origin of the name. One has it named after well-known peaks in the Cook and Society groups of islands at which the Māori called on their way to New Zealand.

Then there is a legend connected with the arrival of the famous Ārai-te-uru canoe, which came from Hawaiki in the fourteenth century. The canoe was wrecked and the crew travelled by land northwards through the Mackenzie country. When they sighted Mount Cook they noticed that it was higher than any of the other peaks, which had been named after members of the party. They looked round them to see who was the tallest so that his name might be given to the mountain, and it was found that this was a little boy named Aorangi, who was being carried on the shoulders of his grandfather.

There is another story, which goes back to the time when the gods were to be found on the earth. Some of the sky children came to earth in a canoe, called Te Waka-a-Aorangi (the canoe of Aorangi). The canoe was turned to stone and became the South Island. Aorangi, the captain of the canoe, was turned into the mountain we know as Mount Cook. He had three brothers, Rangi-roa, Rangi-rua, and Rārangi-roa. They were turned into Mounts Dampier and Teichelmann, and the Silberhorn.

The name is applied to many other parts of New Zealand and sometimes it has an entirely different origin. There is a place of this name near Feilding. The famous explorer Tamatea called here on his way to Wanganui. He left a lizard there and called the place Aorangi; it is possible that it was named after the lizard.

The Aorangi Range is misnamed, as it was originally Haurangi. The pronunciation of the two names is very similar.

Mount Cook/Aorangi, the cloud in the sky.

Aorere *ao* (cloud or mist); *rere* (flying). Flying scud or mist. Modern Māori call an aeroplane *ao-rere* or *manu-rere* (flying bird).

Aoroa *ao* (cloud); *roa* (long). Long cloud.

Aotea The name of the canoe in which Turi came

to New Zealand. The Aotea gave its name to a small harbour on the west coast of the North Island where the immigrants first landed. It was also the Māori name of Great Barrier Island.

There is a farming district in Marlborough which was named Aotea by Archdeacon Grace because it means sunny spot.

Aotearoa The usual meaning given to the Māori name for New Zealand is Land of the long white cloud. *Ao* (cloud); *tea* (white); *roa* (long). But this is only one of several possible meanings. The following interpretations have been given by various authorities: Long white cloud; Continuously clear light; Big glaring light; Land of abiding day; Long white world; Long bright world; Long daylight; Long lingering day; Long bright land; Long bright day. Most of these meanings can be justified because *ao* means both cloud and day, and *tea* both white and bright.

According to legend, when Kupe, the first discoverer of New Zealand, first came in sight of the land, his wife cried, 'He ao! He ao!' ('A cloud! A cloud!'). Great Barrier Island was therefore named Aotea (white cloud), and the long mainland Aotearoa (long white cloud). When Kupe finally returned to his homeland his people asked him why he did not call the newly discovered country after his fatherland. He replied, 'I preferred the warm breast to the cold one, the new land to the old land long forsaken.'

Nevertheless the name still provides some problems which may never be fully solved.

Aotuhia *ao* (daylight); *tuhia* (to glow). Glowing daylight.

Aowhenua *ao* (daylight); *whenua* (land or country). Land of daylight.

Aparima *apa* (a party of workmen); *rima* (five). The name is almost certainly that of a celebrated Waitaha chieftainess of long ago. Another theory gives the name as the Māori form of Apolima, an island in the Pacific known to Māori before the migration.

There is an interesting but dubious conjecture that the name means 'fivefold streams' or 'fivefold ridges'. From five ridges the Aparima River receives five tributaries, which are known as the Five Rivers district.

Āpiti Narrow pass or gorge.

Apoka This small inlet in Marlborough is named after a Māori, Ihone Apoka, who lived there.

Aponga Gathered together or heaped up.

Ara-a-Kiwa The path of Kiwa. The Māori name for Foveaux Strait. Kiwa was an ocean god.

Moonrise, looking over Foveaux Strait or Ara-a-Kiwa, from Halfmoon Bay, Stewart Island.

Arahiwi *ara* (track or path); *hiwi* (ridge or hill-top). A descriptive name. Path over the ridge.

Arahura *ara* (path); *hura* (to discover). The name is connected with Ngahue, who was the companion of Kupe on his discovery of New Zealand. Ara'ura is the ancient name of Aitutaki in the Cook Islands, and the landing place and river in the South Island were possibly named in memory of the island home.

On the other hand, it may be that Kupe and Ngahue, after a battle with an octopus in Cook Strait, went down to the West Coast of the South

Island to see if any people lived there. Ngahue gave the name to commemorate their search. Arahura was also an early name for the South Island.

Ārai Screen or veil.

Ārai-te-uru The name of the early canoe which was wrecked at Moeraki. Originally applied to Shag Point.

Arakihi *ara* (path); *kihi* (to be cut off).

Aramatai *ara* (path); *matai* (native tree). The path indicated by a matai tree.

Okiwa Bay from the Picton-Havelock Road, Queen Charlotte Sound.

Aramiro *ara* (path); *miro* (native tree). This and the previous name may indicate that a path was made across a stream by felling a tree.

Aramoana *ara* (path); *moana* (ocean).

Aramoho The correct form is Aramuhu. *Ara* (path); *muhu* (to force one's way through heavy bush). A Māori named Hau-e-rangi was lost in the dense bush here and wandered about until he died of starvation. When his body was found it was seen that he had beaten an almost circular path in his struggle to find a way out.

Aranga The act of rising.

Aranui The origin of this name varies for different places. In Christchurch it was probably from *ara* (path); *nui* (big).

The Aranui Cave at Waitomo was named after a Māori who discovered it while pig-hunting. The Aranui Creek on the West Coast derives from *ara* (a small freshwater fish); *nui* (many). Large

numbers of grayling were taken in this creek by the Māori.

Arapaepae *ara* (path); *paepae* (ridge). Path along a ridge.

Arapaoa *ara* (path); *paoa* (smoke, or blow). The name is an interesting one, of importance in Māori tradition. Not only is it the correct form of Arapawa Island, but it was also once used for the whole of the South Island, and later for the island that Captain Cook landed on to discover Cook Strait. It received its name in one of two ways. It was close to the entrance of Queen Charlotte Sound, where Kupe with a downward blow (paoa) killed the enormous octopus Muturangi. The second theory is that early Māori peered through the mist across the strait which they called 'the misty path'.

Arapawa *ara* (path); *Pawa* (name of Kupe's slave). Arapawa Island, however, is correctly spelt Arapaoa, q.v.

Arapawa Island.

Arapito *ara* (path); *pito* (end). The Māori travelled along a well-used track by the Karamea River inland to snare birds and gather berries. The track ended at a point where the present settlement of Arapito stands.

Arapōhue *ara* (path); *pōhue* (convolvulus plant). Path through the convolvulus.

Arapuni *ara* (path); *puni* (blocked, or place of encampment). The meaning may be Path to the camp, a path that has been blocked up by some obstruction.

Ararātā *ara* (path); *rātā* (native tree). Path by or through rātā trees.

Ararimu *ara* (path); *rimu* (native tree). Path by or through rimu trees.

Ararua *ara* (path); *rua* (two). Two paths.

Arataha *ara* (path); *taha* (to pass by).

Aratapu *ara* (path); *tapu* (sacred, or prohibited). The sacred path, or Path to a sacred place. The full name is Te Aratapu-o-Manaia. Manaia was a chief who came to New Zealand in the Tokomaru canoe in the thirteenth or fourteenth century and landed here on the Wairoa River, Kaipara.

Aratāura Probably derived from *ara* (path); *tāuru* (head or source of a stream). Path by the source of a stream.

Aratiatia *ara tiatia* (a series of pegs stuck into the ground to assist in climbing a steep ascent). This descriptive name has been applied to the rapids on the Waikato River because the water seems to zig-zag from one rock to another like the primitive ladders used by Māori. It may also be connected with the explorer Tia, who proceeded up the rapids in his small canoe. It is said that the old river bed was a series of small ledges, each of which carried Tia past another obstacle as he paddled up it.

Aratika *ara* (path); *tika* (straight). Direct path.

Aratoro *ara* (path); *toro* (to explore, to discover).

Arawhata This may mean a hanging path. A whata is a food-store elevated on a post to keep the contents away from rats. Such stores were sometimes approached by a notched post which was leant against the store, thus providing a series of steps or stairs. Such a stairway was known as an arawhata, a path to the food-store.

Arero Tongue. There is a tradition that there was a battle here, and that the victors cut out the tongues of the vanquished.

Āria A deep pool, or a stretch of water suitable for fishing by net.

Ariki-kapakapa *ariki* is short for *puna-ariki* (hot springs); *kapakapa* (flapping). The name refers to the flapping or fluttering noise made by the hot spring.

Aroaro-kaihe The Māori name for Mount Sefton. Aroaro-kaihe and her husband Mauka-tū (Ben Ohou) were both members of the crew of the Ārai-te-uru canoe.

The Ben Ohau Range.

Aropaoanui *aro* (fat covering the kidneys); *paoa nui* (thoroughly bashed). The pā at the mouth of the Aropaoanui River was raided, but the defenders were victorious. In order to celebrate their victory a great feast was prepared with the bodies of the slain. When the ovens were opened up and the cooks were watching the bodies, something happened that caused them to run away in fright and horror. They had seen the bodies moving. They told their chief, Rākai, what they had seen, and he realised at once that it was the kidney fat which was twitching. He went to the ovens and paoa nui (thoroughly bashed) the offending portions. From this incident the place received its name.

Arorangi *aro* (front); *rangi* (heaven). The front of heaven. The name was brought from the island of Tahiti.

Arowhenua *aro* (face or front); *whenua* (land). Several interpretations have been given from time to time, including Good or desirable land; Turning up land for cultivation; and To face or desire land. It is an ancient Polynesian name transplanted to New Zealand.

Ātaahua Good, beautiful, or pleasant.

Atapō *ata* (shadow); *pō* (night). Night shadows.

Atarau Moon, or moonlight.

Atawhai Liberality, or kindness.

Ātea Space. A synonym for Watea, the personified form of space.

Ātene The Māori form of Athens. The name was given to the mission station on the Whanganui River by the Reverend Richard Taylor, the original Māori name being O-a-whiti.

Ātiamuri It was at the Ātiamuri Rapids that Tia, the elder brother of the commander of the Arawa canoe, turned back. The name therefore can be broken up into the words Ā-Tia-muri, muri here meaning 'turned back'.

It has also been conjectured that the word is a contraction of the tribal name Ngāti-a-Muri.

Atiu One of the oldest names in Marlborough, it has probably been transferred from the Cook Islands.

Auripo Both *au* and *ripo* mean whirlpool or swirling current.

Auroa *au* (cloud, mist, or current); *roa* (long).

Awaawaroa *awaawa* (valley); *roa* (long). Long valley.

Awahonu *awa* (river); *honu* (deep). Deep river.

Awahou *awa* (river); *hou* (new). New river. The Awahou River, which flows into Lake Rotorua, was named by the explorer Ihenga.

Awahuri *awa* (river); *huri* (fascine to turn fish into a river). River with a weir in it.

Awaiti *awa* (stream); *iti* (small). The place of this name in Awarua Bay, Nelson, once provided a problem when a post office was opened. It could not be called Awarua because there was another post office of that name. There were two rivers in the bay, the larger being called Awanui (big river). It was then decided to call the other Awaiti (little river).

Awakaponga *awa* (stream); *kaponga* (tree-fern). Tree-fern stream.

Awakari *awa* (river); *kari* (isolated clump of trees).

River with isolated patches of bush on the banks.

Awakeri Ditch.

Awakino *awa* (river); *kino* (bad). Bad river. The Awakino River is still muddy in places, which possibly gave rise to the name.

Awakōkōmuka See under Awamoa.

Awamangu *awa* (river); *mangu* (black). Black river.

Awamarino *awa* (river); *marino* (calm). Calm river.

Awamate *awa* (river); *mate* (dead). Dead river, or Former river. At Awamate in Nelson, a branch of the Motueka River used to run through the place which bore this name.

Awamoa *awa* (stream); *moa* (large, extinct flightless bird). Moa stream. The name was given by W.B.D. Mantell in about 1852. The original name was Awakōkōmuka. *Awa* (stream); *kōkōmuka* (the South Island name for *koromiko*: a native species of veronica). At the mouth of the stream Mantell discovered ancient ovens of the Waitaha tribe containing moa bones. The stones of the ovens were heated by burning kōkōmuka, which was considered the best fuel for the purpose. Mantell preferred to call the stream by the more euphonious and appropriate name, Awamoa.

Awamōkihi *awa* (river); *mōkihi* (a craft made of flax sticks). The stream north of Ōamaru was named after a man called Awamōkihi.

Awamoko *awa* (stream); *moko* (lizard). Lizard stream.

Awanga South-west wind, or a variety of flax or taro.

Awanui *awa* (river); *nui* (large, or many). The name may have been brought from Hawaiki.

Awapuni *awa* (river); *puni* (blocked up). It has been suggested that the river may have been blocked up with driftwood when it was named.

There was a lagoon called Te Awa-puni at Palmerston North, which was an ox-bow or cut-off river bend, and could thus be described as a blocked river.

Awapūtakitaki *awa* (river): *pūtakitaki* (the South Island form of *pūtangitangi*: Paradise duck).

Awarere *awa* (river); *rere* (flowing). Flowing river.

Awariki *awa* (river); *riki* (small). Small river.

Awaroa *awa* (river); *roa* (long). Long river.

Awarua *awa* (river); *rua* (two). Two rivers, or arms. The name is a common one in New Zealand and throughout Polynesia. Avarua is the name of a harbour in Ra'iatea, which had two openings in the reef.

Awatea Daylight, or midday.

Awatere *awa* (river); *tere* (swift flowing). Swift-flowing river. Of the river at East Cape it is said that in a battle one man had his stomach ripped open, and the contents ran swiftly down the current, hence the name.

   The name may be the true form of Kawatiri.

Awatoitoi *awa* (river); *toitoi* (a small freshwater fish, a variety of flax, or possibly a corruption of *toetoe*).

Awatoto *awa* (river); *toto* (blood, or the name of a ceremony performed over a child, usually by the side of a stream).

Awatuna *awa* (creek); *tuna* (eel). Eel creek. The settlement of this name in Taranaki is known locally as Eels Creek.

Āwhitu Longing to return. Literally the meaning of āwhitu is to feel regret for, to yearn for. At one time the Māori at this settlement near the heads of the Manukau Harbour were forced to abandon their pā because of the depredations of the taniwha Kaiwhare, and they took the title Te Rua-o-Kaiwhare. It has been suggested that the place was named because of their longing to return to familiar surroundings and the place they loved.

E

Eaheinōmāuwe This is Captain Cook's spelling of the Māori name for the North Island. It probably stands for *He ahi nō Māui* (The fire of Māui), and refers to the volcanoes of the Central Plateau.

E Kapa A modern name, after a Māori who lived here.

Ekemānuka *eke* (to crouch); *mānuka* (tea-tree shrub). A party of Māori who were out hunting saw a large enemy force approaching. They made their escape unseen by crouching down and creeping through the short mānuka scrub.

Eketāhuna *eke* (to run aground); *tāhuna* (shoal or sandbank). This place was as far as the Makakahi River could be navigated by canoes on account of the shoals.

Epuni Correctly, Te Puni. He was the Ngāti-Awa chief who greeted Wakefield and his companions when the *Tory* arrived off Petone beach. E Puni! is the vocative form of address, meaning O Puni!

Erua Two. The *e* is a particle used before digits one to nine in enumeration, e.g. e rua, e toru, two, three. Another ingenious explanation of the name has been offered in the form E rua!, which could be translated colloquially, 'Hello, there's a cave!'

Mount Ngāuruhoe from Erua.

Haehaenui *haehae* (to lacerate, or parallel grooves in a carving); *nui* (big). An ingenious but doubtful theory is that this is the original name for the Arrow River; it means 'big scratches' — a reference to the number of channels the river has carved.

Haere-huka *haere* (to come or go); *huka* (foam). The name was apparently applied to the great rock in the middle of the Huka rapids. It has been popularly translated Moving foam, or Flying foam.

Hairini Possibly the Māori form of Ireland, but more probably it is a missionary name, Cyrene, which takes this form in Māori.

Hakahaka The name of a Marlborough chief.

Hakakura *haka* (a South Island form of *whanga*, a hollow); *kura* (red). Reddish-coloured hollow. It is the original Māori name for Lake Sumner.

Hākana This bay at Port Underwood is, in a roundabout way, probably named after the pioneer missionary the Reverend Samuel Ironside. He was known to Māori as Haeana, which was the nearest they could get to the pronunciation. Hākana is thought to be a corruption of Haeana.

Hakapōua *haka* (a South Island form of *whanga* a hollow); *pōua* (old man). It is thought that the Māori used the expression 'old man' in much the same way as Pākehā might say 'old man flood'. The name has therefore been jocularly translated as Grandfather's Gully, Old Man Gulf, and Big Chasm of the Aged Man.

Hakapūpū *haka* (South Island form of harbour); *pūpū* (several kinds of shellfish). Estuary of the shellfish.

Haka-pūreirei *haka* (dance); *pureirei* (tufts of grass, or small patch of garden).

Hakarū *haka* (dance); *rū* (to shake).

Te Arawa men perform a haka.

Hakataramea *haka* (dance); *taramea* (spear-grass). The name commemorates a dance which took place near the mouth of the river. The performers wore bags filled with the sweet-scented gum from the flower stalks of the taramea. The bags in which the gum was contained were made from the skin of the whekau, an owl that is now extinct.

Flowering harakeke.

Hakatere *haka* (a form of *whaka*: to make); *tere* (swift). To make swift. It is the Māori name for the Ashburton River.

Hāmama To shout aloud. Three young men from Taumarunui came down the Whanganui River to kill a chief named Tama-tuna. Caught by surprise, Tama-tuna shouted out loudly. He was killed and his wives insulted.

Hamaria A missionary village on the shore of Lake Taupo, named after the biblical town of Samaria.

Hamurana The Māori form of the biblical name Smyrna, given to the springs at Rotorua, which were originally called Te Puna-a-Hangarua. See under Hangarua.

Hangaroa An ornamental belt, anklet, or necklace made of shells.

Hangarua A name occasionally given to the Hamurana Springs, (see under Hamurana). The full name is Te Puna-a-Hangarua, meaning The spring of Hangarua. It was presided over by a taniwha or water monster named Hinerua. The small blind fish, kōaro, which came up in the waters of the spring from time to time, were called the Children of Hinerua.

Hangatiki *hanga* (to fashion or make); *tiki* (an image in human form). To carve a wooden post in the form of a tiki.

Hāparangi To shout, or to cut open.

Hāpua A hollow or pool.

Hāpuawhenua *hāpua* (depression); *whenua* (land).

Hāpuku The fish known to Pākehā as groper.

Harakeke Flax (*Phormium tenax*).

Harihari A song to make people pull together in unison.

Hātaitai Many meanings are given for the name of this Wellington suburb. The most interesting is the myth that two taniwha once lived in the lake which is now Wellington Harbour. They attempted to force their way out. One, Ngake, succeeded and made the entrance to the harbour. The other, Whātaitai, failed. He changed into a bird and flew screaming to the top of Mount Victoria (Tangi-te-keo). The suburb should therefore be named Whātaitai.

There have been attempts to provide a literal translation. *Hā* (smell or breath) or *whā* (to cause or make known); *taitai* (tide), resulting in such meanings as The lapping of the tide, or The breath of the ocean.

Hātepe To cut off, or to proceed in an orderly manner.

Hātuma Possibly a personal name. It was sometimes called Whātuma. No meaning can be ascribed, but an old Māori once stated that it referred to the discoverers of the lake who ate until they were satisfied. The name was given by Tara.

Hauhangaroa *hau* (wind); *hangaroa* (seashells).

Haumaitikitiki Also in the form Haumātiketike, it was applied to mountains such as Mount Brewster, Mount Prospect, and the Crown Range. The name is descriptive, meaning The wind blowing from the heights.

The Crown Range, Haumaitikitiki.

Haumātakitaki Named after a chieftainess of Otago.

Haumoana *hau* (wind); *moana* (ocean). Sea breeze.

Haunui *hau* (wind); *nui* (big). Strong wind.

Haupapa *hau* (wind); *papa* (flat). Windy flat.

Hauraki *hau* (wind); *raki* (north). Northern wind. There is a proverb about Hauraki which refers to a wind that rises moaning from the sea. No doubt this is the north wind. It has been said, however, that Hauraki (or Haurangi) was a personal name.

Hauroko *hau* (wind); *roko* (South Island form of *rongo*: sound). Sound of the wind. This is the meaning ascribed to it by Southland Māori, and the name has been officially noted as Hauroko. But it has been the subject of dispute in the past, for it is held by some northern Māori that it should be Hauroto. *Hau* (wind); *roto* (lake). Windy lake.

Hautapu *hau* (there are many meanings; here it possibly refers to a religious ceremony); *tapu* (sacred). Sacred ceremony.

Hautekapakapa *hau* (wind); *te* (the); *kapakapa* (flapping). The flapping of the wind.

Hautere *hau* (wind); *tere* (swift). Swift wind.

Hauturu *hau* (wind); *turu* (post). Wind's resting-post. This is the Māori name for Little Barrier Island. In legend it is one of the centre posts of the great net of Taramainuku. For an account of this net, see under Te Kupenga-a-Taramainuku.

Hauwai A mollusc.

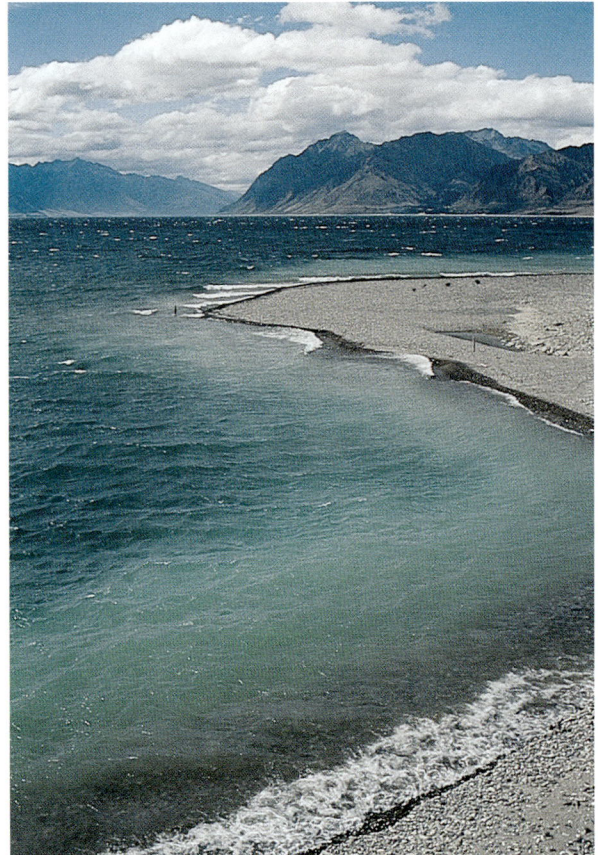

Lake Hawea.

Hāwea The Hāwea tribe were among the original inhabitants of the South Island. The lake and other places where the name occurs may be named originally from one of Rākai-haitū's men. If the name was given through some event in history, it implies doubt and indecision.

Hāwera *hā* (breath); *wera* (hot, or burnt). Breath of fire. The occupants of a crowded whare were attacked by their enemies here, and the house was set on fire. The people who were inside were killed by 'the breath of fire'.

He ahi nō Māui An ancient name for the North Island. See under Eaheinōmāuwe.

Heipipi *hei* (necklace); *pipi* (shellfish). Necklace of pipi.

Hekeia The father of Te Anau, one of the early immigrants from Hawaiki.

Hekura The name of a woman of the Ārai-te-uru canoe.

Hemo To cease, or disappear.

Herekino *here* (knot); *kino* (bad). Badly tied knot.

Heretaunga *here* (to tie); *taunga* (to come to rest, applied to a canoe). But Heretaunga of the Hutt Valley was never a suitable place for canoes. It has been suggested that it is a corruption of Hautonga, breath of the south wind. There is also a theory that the name was imported from Hawke's Bay. The Heretaunga Plains were named after a notable carved house built near present-day Hastings by Whātonga.

Hiapo The famous sisters Kuiwai and Haungaroa left their brother Hiapo here while they went to Maketū to carry messages from Hawaiki to Ngātoro-i-rangi.

Hihitahi *hihi* (stitch-bird); *tahi* (single). A single stitch-bird.

Hikuai This may be a contraction of Hikuwai, one meaning of which is Tail end of the backwash. *Hiku* (fish's tail); *wai* (water).

Hikurangi The name appears in many parts of New Zealand, because it commemorates a well-known and loved mountain peak in Hawaiki. The probable meaning is *hiku* (point, or summit); *rangi* (sky).

Hikutaiā *hiku* (tail, or end); *taiā* (neap tide). Tail end of the tide.

Hīmatangi *hī* (to fish with hook and line); *Matangi* (the name of a chief). Matangi's fishing. At one time it was thought that the name was really Hima-tangi, referring to the weeping (*tangi*) of Hima for her lost greenstone treasure. But the story is now believed to relate to the chief Matangi, who settled here long ago. Travellers were killed by a huge taniwha in a lake by the Manawatū River and Matangi set out with twelve men to kill it. Some of them acted as bait, tempting the taniwha from its home. Others lay in wait and snared it with ropes when it emerged, then killed it.

Hinahina A native tree.

Hinakura The name of a chieftainess who took ill and died by the Pahaoa River. She was buried there and the place was named after her. The correct form of the name is Hinekura.

Hīnau A native tree.

Hinerua *hine* (girl); *rua* (two). Two girls.

Hine-te-awa *hine* (girl); *te* (the); *awa* (river). The girl of the river. This is the original name of Bowen Falls, which are named after a woman who lived long ago.

Hine-te-awa or Bowen Falls.

Hinuera Correctly, Hinuwera. *Hinu* (oil, or fat); *wera* (burning). Burning fat or oil.

Hiona A missionary name for a pā on the Whanganui River. It is the Māori form of Zion.

Hira Abundant, or multitude.

Hiruhārama Māori form of Jerusalem. Named by the Reverend Richard Taylor.

Hītaua A small waist-mat or apron.

Hiwinui *hiwi* (ridge); *nui* (big). Big ridge.

Hiwipango Correctly, Hiwiponga. *Hiwi* (ridge); *ponga* (tree-fern). Ridge covered with tree-ferns.

Hoe-o-Tainui

Hoe-o-Tainui *hoe* (paddle); *o* (of); *Tainui* (the Tainui canoe). Paddle of the Tainui canoe.

Hōhonu Deep. A suitable name for the river.

Hokianga It is from here that Kupe the navigator returned to Hawaiki. From this event the place was named Hokianga, Great returning place of Kupe. It is said that the correct form is Hoki-anga-nui (direct return), or Hokianga-nui-a-Kupe.

Hōkio Whistling. Hau gave the name because the wind whistled in his ears.

Hokitika *hoki* (to return); *tika* (directly, or in a straight line). When some of Ngāi-Tahu were about to attack the pā here, one or more of their chiefs were drowned, and they therefore made a direct return back to their home. Bishop Harper once wrote that the name means '"When you get there, turn back again", as the Māori regard it as the end of the earth'.

The Hokitika River.

Hokonui There are two explanations. First, that *hoko* is a contraction of *hokowhitu* (war party); *nui* (large). Large war party. Second, that Hokonui is a corruption of *hukanui*. *Huka* (snow); *nui* (big). Thick snow.

Hokowhitu War party of about 140 men. Hokowhitu near Palmerston North was so named because of the men who garrisoned at Te Motu-o-Poutoa.

Homai To give to the person speaking.

Hongihongi To smell. Turi of the Aotea canoe took up a handful of earth at this place and smelled it to see whether the soil was good.

Hongi's Point The pā Kororipo, where Hongi Hika carried the bodies of chiefs slain in battle, was here.

Hongi's Track Where Hongi took his canoes overland in 1822 from Rotoehu to Rotoiti on his way to attack Mokoia Island. The Māori name is Te Ara-a-Hongi.

Honikiwi *honi* (to nibble, or eat); *kiwi* (native flightless bird). Where the kiwi forages for food.

Horahora Greatly expanded, or scattered about.

Hōreke To throw a spear.

Horoeka A native tree (lancewood).

Horoera *horo* (to swallow); *wera* (hot). To swallow hot.

Horohoro The name in full is Te Horohoroinga-o-ngā-ringaringa-a-Tia, The place where Tia's hands were ceremonially washed. This was necessary to remove the tapu after handling the dead. Tia was the Arawa explorer who named Lake Taupo.

An alternative for the full name is Te Horohoronga-a-Tia, which refers to the swallowing of sacred food in a ceremony to remove tapu.

Horoirangi *horoi* (to wash, or cleanse); *rangi* (sky). When bad weather threatens Nelson, this mountain is covered with clouds.

Horokiwi *horo* (to run); *kiwi* (native flightless bird). The running of the kiwi.

Horokōau *horo* (to swallow); *kōau* (shag). Te Horokōau is probably Mount Tasman, and is said to have been given this name because it resembled the swelling in the long neck of a shag when it is swallowing a fish. The name appears in several places in the South Island.

It is also the name for the Cass River, and could there be interpreted as A precipitous landslip (*horo*) where shags congregated.

Horokōhatu *horo* (crumbling); *kōhatu* (stone). Crumbling stone. It may be an adaptation of the name Te Horokoatu, who was on the Ārai-te-uru canoe.

Horokōau or Mount Tasman.

Horopito A native shrub (the pepper tree). The literal meaning is Scent of the woods.

Hororātā *horo* (landslip); *rātā* (native tree).

Horotiu *horo* (to run); *tiu* (swift). Swiftly flowing. Above the junction of the Waipā, the Waikato River flowed swiftly. Until after the Waikato War the name Waikato was used only for the river below Ngāruawāhia; above it was termed the Horotiu.

Horotutu *horo* (landslip); *tutu* (native tree).

Horowhenua *horo* (slip); *whenua* (land). Great landslide. The whole district from Levin to the Ōhau River is a gravel deposit. It is a fan of detritus which has the appearance of an enormous landslide from the Tararua Range.

Hōteo A calabash.

Houhora *hou* (feather); *hora* (to spread out). Feathers spread out. Feathers were at one time spread out near the Houhora Heads to dry.

Houhou A native tree (five-finger).

Houhou-pounamu *houhou* (to drill); *pounamu* (greenstone). To drill greenstone. This stream near Greytown was named from the custom of drilling greenstone and using the water of the stream in the process.

Houipapa *houi* (lacebark or ribbonwood tree); *papa* (flat). Ribbonwood flat. This is the name used by Pākehā.

Houpoto *hou* (feather); *poto* (short). Short feather.

Hōuto Ripe fruit of the poporo tree.

Huapai *hua* (fruit); *pai* (good). Good fruit. This settlement was founded and named in 1912. It is a noted fruit-growing district.

Huarau *hua* (fruit); *rau* (hundred, or many). Plentiful fruit.

Huatai *hua* (product, or progeny); *tai* (tide). The name means Sea froth.

Hūhūtahi *hūhū* (thigh); *tahi* (single). Only thigh. One of Tama-tū-pere's thighs was eaten at this place, on which the settlement of Rānana was later established.

Huia An extinct native bird, the feathers of which were greatly prized. It was never known to be in the Karamea district (the Huia River is a tributary of the Karamea). The name was probably conferred by an early surveyor.

Huiarau *huia* (extinct native bird); *rau* (many). Many huia birds.

Huihui-kōura *huihui* (assembly); *kōura* (crayfish). Gathering of crayfish. Old Māori tell stories of walls of crayfish plastered solidly several tiers deep in the waters of Stevens Island, in Breaksea Sound.

Huinga Said to mean swamps.

Huiroa A species of fine flax.

Hui te Rangiora Name of the great explorer and navigator of the seventh century, who is reputed to have sailed down to the Antarctic in his canoe. The district adjoining the mouth of Motueka River was named after him.

Huka Foam. The name of the great waterfall on the Waikato River below Lake Taupo is Hukanui in full.

Hukanui *huka* (foam, spray, or snow); *nui* (big). Great body of foam.

Hukapapa *huka* (snow, or frost); *papa* (flat). Frosty flat.

Hukarere *huka* (spray, or foam); *rere* (flying). Flying foam. This was the high seaward bluff of

Hūkerenui

Scinde Island, Napier, and in storms the spray would come right to the hilltop at this point.

Huka Falls.

Hūkerenui *hūkere* (cascade); *nui* (big). Great cascade.

Hūnua Infertile, high country.

Huriawa *huri* (to turn round); *awa* (river). River turned round. The Waikouaiti River once entered the sea on the south side of the Huriawa Peninsula into Puketeraki Bay.

Hurimoana *huri* (to overflow); *moana* (ocean). Overflowing sea.

Huri-o-te-wai *huri* (to turn round); *o* (of); *te* (the); *wai* (water). The dividing of the water. This is the Māori name for Bishop's Peninsula on Pepin Island, which diverts the Whakapuaka stream from the tide.

Huritini *huri* (to revolve); *tini* (many). Ever circulating, or Many circles. It is a large pool of boiling muddy water at Tikitere.

Huruhuru-o-Taikawa *huruhuru* (coarse hair); *o* (of); *Taikawa* (name of a chieftainess). The local meaning, however, is The soft hair of Taikawa. She insisted that the muka or dressed flax of this part of Horowhenua was so fine that it should be called by this name.

Hurunui *huru* (hair); *nui* (big). One explanation is that the name means Flowing hair. It does have something of this appearance from the hills. It may have taken its name from the female dog, Hurunui, which Kupe was supposed to have left in charge of his discoveries. It may also refer to vegetation by the banks.

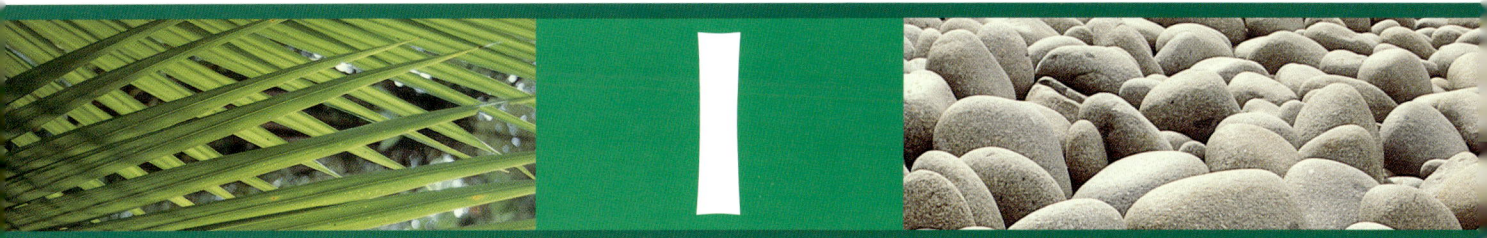

Ihu-ngau-anā *ihu* (nose): *ngau* (bite); *anā* (there). Nose bitten off. A chief named Tama-haki had his nose bitten off by Kura at a battle here on the Whanganui River.

The Whanganui River.

Ikamatua *ika* (fish); *matua* (parent, or fully grown). One explanation of the name is that it is a shortened form of Te Ika-a-matua, The fish of my ancestor (Māui).

Ikoraki A South Island form of Hikurangi.

Inangahua *inanga* (whitebait); *hua* (preserved by drying in the sun, or plenty of). The Inangahua River was noted for the big catches of whitebait that it yielded.

Irimahuwheri The correct name of this headland in the Buller district is Irimahuwhero. *Iri* (hanging); *mahu* (hair); *whero* (red). Hanging red hair. On the seaward side of the headland there are masses of rātā trees, which are sometimes ablaze with red blooms.

Iwikatea *iwi* (bone); *katea* (bleached). Bleached bones. This is the Māori name for the site of Balclutha. A great battle took place here long ago, and the bones remained for many years.

Iwirua *iwi* (bone); *rua* (pit, or cave). There may have been a burial ground on this cape in Grove Arm, Marlborough Sounds.

Iwituaroa Backbone. From the sea the Iwituaroa Range bears a striking resemblance to a human backbone.

K

Kāeo Freshwater shellfish.

Kaharoa *kaha* (net); *roa* (long). Large seine or dragnet.

Kahika Native tree. Short for Kahikatea (white pine).

Kahikatea White pine. Kahikatea Bay was an early name for Curious Cove.

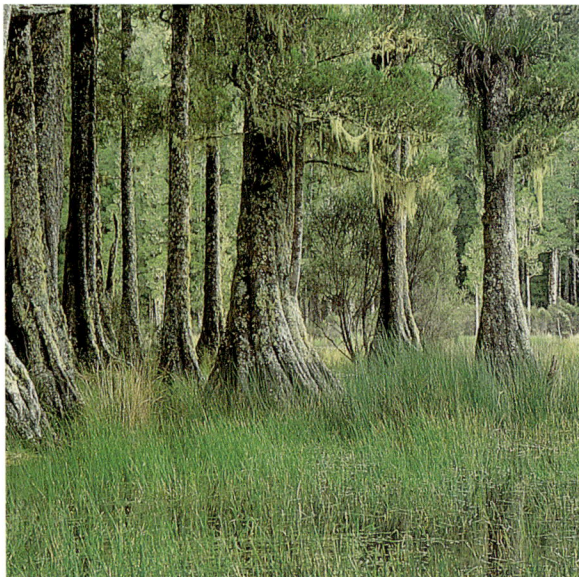

A stand of kahikatea, central North Island.

Kahinu This peak in the Tararua Range was named after a chief of the Rangitāne pā.

Kahiwiroa *kahiwi* (ridge); *roa* (long). Long ridge.

Kahu Named after Kahu-mata-momoe, son of Tama-te-kapua, because he stayed here at Ōrakei in Auckland.

Kāhui Flock, or herd.

Kāhuika The meeting of the waters. It is the equivalent of the North Island Ngāhuinga, and describes the meeting of the Matau and Clutha Rivers.

Kāhui-kākāpō *kāhui* (meeting); *kākāpō* (ground parrot). 'Kākāpō Parliament'. An old legend says that Doubtful Sound was a place where the chief of the kākāpō sent out invitations to his subjects to meet together to discuss matters of common interest among the parrots. Spey River and Hall's Arm were similar meeting places.

Kāhui-kau-peka Assembly of river-heads. The Māori name for D'Archiac, which is the source of many rivers.

Kāhui-kawau *kāhui* (assembly); *kawau* (shag). Assembly of shags. Ihenga's wife exclaimed with delight at the many birds he had brought in his canoe, so the place, between Rotorua and Maketū, was given this name.

Kāhuitamariki *kāhui* (assembly); *tamariki* (grandchildren). Assembly of grandchildren.

Doubtful Sound.

Kahukura Rainbow, or god of the rainbow.

Kahuranaki Properly, Kahura-a-nake, the wished for. When the Māori set out from Wairoa to Ahuriri in their canoes, this high hill was their landmark. If it became obscured by clouds, it was greatly wished for.

Kahurangi *kahu* (blue); *rangi* (sky). Blue skies. Canoe voyagers from the North Island, Nelson and Marlborough always endeavoured to reach the mouth of the Kahurangi River in the evening, because this landfall was almost invariably associated with blue skies and calm waters.

Kahutara The name of one of the canoes in which the Māori came to New Zealand. The Ngāi-Tahu came from the North Island in a canoe with the same name and established themselves here, a little south of Kaikōura.

Kahuwera *kahu* (garment); *wera* (burnt). Burnt garment. The Māori village in the Bay of Islands was so named because a woman's garment caught fire here, and she had to rush into the sea to extinguish it. The same name in Southland comes from the name of a woman who lived there about 300 years ago.

Kaiaka Adept, or man.

Kaiapoi It is generally agreed that the correct form of the name is Kaiapohia, meaning food depot. But some South Island Māori deny this, and say that it has always been Kaiapoi. *Kai* (food); *poi* (swung). The pā was in a strategic position and adequate food supplies could be 'swung' towards it from all directions.

Kaiarero *kai* (to bite, or eat); *arero* (tongue). Bite the tongue.

Kaiata *kai* (food); *ata* (morning). Eat in the morning.

Kaiate *kai* (food); *ate* (liver). Meal of liver. The livers of sharks were often eaten here.

Kaiaua *kai* (to eat); *aua* (herring). Meal of herring.

Kai-hau-o-Kupe *kai* (eating); *hau* (wind); *o* (of); *Kupe* (the famous explorer). Kupe's wind-eating. When Kupe stayed at this spot at Castlecliff it was very windy.

Kaihere *kai* (food); *here* (to tie).

Kaihiku *kai* (to eat); *hiku* (tail of a fish). To eat fish-tails.

Kaihinu *kai* (food); *hinu* (fat). Rich food.

Kaihū The full name was Kai-hū-a-Ihenga. *Kai* (food); *hū* (secret); *a* (of); *Ihenga* (grandson of Tama-te-kapua). Ihenga went travelling in the far north, and his men carried some toheroa inland. While his companions were absent, he ate all the remaining supplies, and pretended he knew nothing about it. He was found out, and the place named as a reminder of his greed.

Kai-iwi *kai* (number); *iwi* (tribe). Gathering of the tribes. Several meanings have been advanced. Kai also means eat, and iwi means bone. One of the stories is that a chief ate the flesh and bones of birds; and another is that food of bone was threat against an enemy tribe. It is also said that a woman named Hine-koatu was killed and eaten, and her bones thrown into the stream. And there is an amusing tale that a woman named Kiteiwi was one day eating a choice morsel of kuia (old woman). Someone asked her what she was eating, and she replied, 'The bone of a kōkako [New Zealand crow]', which was a good joke, and so the place was named Kai-iwi (eat the bone).

Kāika Village. This name, which occurs often in the South Island, is the same as the North Island *kāinga*, an unfortified village.

Kaikanohi *kai* (to eat); *kanohi* (eye). A noted warrior caught his wife with another man and swallowed her eyes as an act of revenge. Thus a point on Ellesmere Spit gained its name. Elsewhere in the South Island the name came from unworked greenstone, and was also the name of a famous mere (club).

Kāikanui *kāika* (village, also *kāinga*); *nui* (big). Big settlement.

Kaikohe *kai* (food); *kohe* (tree, or climbing plant).

Kaikōrai Correctly, Kaikārae. *Kai* (to eat); *kārae* (a sea bird).

Kaikōura *kai* (to eat); *kōura* (crayfish). To eat crayfish. The full name is Te-Ahi-kai-kōura-a-Tama-ki-te-rangi (or Tamatea-pōkai-whenua). This great traveller stayed here and lit a fire to cook a meal of crayfish, and this is what the full name means. The name of this place was once applied to the whole of the South Island.

The Kaikōura coast.

Kaimāī *kai* (to eat); *māī* (mussel). To eat mussels.

Kaimanawa *kai* (to eat); *manawa* (heart). Heart-eater.

Kaimata *kai* (to eat); *mata* (unripe, or uncooked). To eat raw food.

Kaimātaitai *kai* (to eat); *mātaitai* (salty). To eat salty food.

Kaimātuhi *kai* (to eat); *mātuhi* (bush wren). To eat *mātuhi*.

Kaimaumau *kai* (food); *maumau* (wasted). Wasted food.

Kaimiro *kai* (to eat); *miro* (native tree). To eat miro berries.

Kaimoko A man skilled in the art of tattooing. This operation was probably carried out alongside the stream.

Kainamu *kai* (to eat); *namu* (sandfly). To eat sandflies. At this place on the Waiau River a Māori was plagued by sandflies. He licked his hand to allay the itching and inadvertently ate a mouthful of them.

The Sun Trap restaurant, Kaikōura.

Kaingaroa *kainga* (meal); *roa* (long). Protracted meal. The name in full is Te Kaingaroa-a-Haungaroa. A priestess named Haungaroa was exploring the plains. She took so long over her meal that she was teased by her companions, and the place was called The long meal of Haungaroa. The women who made the remark were changed into cabbage trees, which recede across the plain before travellers.

Kaipakatiti *kai* (food); *pakatiti* (defective). Inedible food.

Kaipākirikiri *kai* (food); *pākirikiri* (rock cod). Meal of rock cod.

Kaipara *kai* (to eat); *para* (fern-root). To eat fern-root. When Kahu-mata-momoe and his nephew Ihenga were visiting here, they were well fed, and amongst the food was a basket of para. They had never seen or tasted it before, and named the place after the meal.

Kaipara-te-hau Correctly, Kapara-te-hau. *Kapara* (to sport); *te* (the); *hau* (wind). The wind is sporting. The name probably comes from the chief Te Hau, who was offended by Kupe, who caused the area to be inundated by the sea. It is the shallow lake or lagoon which later became Lake Grassmere.

Kaiparoro *kai* (to eat); *paroro* (bad weather). To eat bad weather. There is a flat-topped hill, and the fogs disappear when they reach it.

Kaipipi *kai* (to eat); *pipi* (shellfish). To eat pipi.

Kaipō *kai* (to eat); *pō* (night). To eat at night.

Kaipuke *kai* (to eat); *puke* (hill). The hill that was eaten. In the old whaling days several ships set out their sails to dry by Kororāreka Point, thus obscuring the hill. Quick to make a joke, the Māori called it Kaipuke.

Kaipūrua *kai* (food); *pūrua* (done in pairs). Fish caught in pairs. A Māori who was fishing in this tributary of the Waiau River caught two fish simultaneously.

Kairanga A company of men making a charge in battle.

Kairara *kai* (food); *rara* (spread out on a platform). Food spread out on a stage.

Kaireperepe *kai* (to eat); *reperepe* (elephant fish). Meal of elephant fish.

Kairua A contraction of Kopukairua. *Kopū* (full); *kai* (food); *rua* (pit). Well-stocked food pit.

Kaitāia In full, Kaitātāia. *Kai* (food); *tātāia* (thrown about). Two women competed to see who could store away the most food. Eventually there was so much gathered together that it could not be contained in the store pits and had to be thrown away.

There is another legend to the effect that Tamatea, son of Rongokako, took vast quantities of wood pigeons here. The name of the place was changed from Orongotea to Kaitāia (food in abundance).

Kaitakata a South Island form of Kaitangata, man-eater. A party of Māori travelling along the beach near Orepuki were overwhelmed by a 'man-eating' wave.

Kaitangata *kai* (to eat); *tangata* (man). The eating of man. After a battle between two tribes over eeling rights on the lakes, the chief Mokomoko was eaten by his victors.

Another account says that the place was named after one of the crew of the Ārai-te-uru canoe, who found a supply of paint in the hills nearby, and was skilled at using it.

Kaitangiweka *kai* (food); *tangi* (to cry); *weka* (wood-hen). The crying of the wood-hen for food.

Kai-tarakihi *kai* (food); *tarakihi* (native fish). Meal of tarakihi. The fishing ground is located by the Māori by sailing out until this mountain comes into view.

Kaitawa *kai* (to eat); *tawa* (native tree).

Kaiteriteri Properly, Kaiteretere *kai* (to eat); *teretere* (quickly). To eat in a hurry. Local Māori who were having a meal on the beach were surprised by stones rolling down the hillside. Fearing a surprise attack, they gathered their food together and ate hurriedly as they retired to the pā.

Stephens Bay, Kaiteriteri.

Kaitī *kai* (to eat); *tī* (cabbage tree). To eat the leaves of the cabbage tree.

Kaitīeke *kai* (to eat); *tieke* (saddleback). To eat the saddleback (native bird).

Kaitoke *kai* (to eat); *toke* (worm). The soil was very poor, and on occasion nothing could be found to eat but worms.

Kaitorete *kai* (to eat); *torete* (parakeet). To eat parakeet. The Ellesmere Spit was a place that had a plentiful supply of birds and fish for food.

Kaituna *kai* (to eat); *tuna* (eel). To eat eels. There were many localities with this name, and no doubt it was a sign that eels abounded and were a popular food.

Kaiuku *kai* (to eat); *uku* (blue clay). To eat clay. The people of this pā were beleaguered, and when their food supplies ran out, they ate clay to assuage their hunger. Their bravery and tenacity were rewarded when a taua came to their aid, the warriors being pulled up the cliff to the pā by ropes.

Kaiumu *kai* (food); *umu* (oven). Food oven.

Kaiwaiwai Correctly, Kaiwaewae. *Kai* (to eat); *waewae* (foot). Destructive to the feet. In the early days the wild Irishman shrub grew plentifully around Featherston, and took its toll on the bare feet of the Māori.

Kaiwaka *kai* (to eat); *waka* (canoe). Destroyer of canoes. Most places where this name is found are by banks of a swiftly running river or stream, which is noted for the canoes 'eaten' or destroyed.

Kaiwharawhara *kai* (to eat); *wharawhara* (fruit of the astelia, which grows in the forks of trees). To eat wharawhara.

Kākā Native parrot.

Kākahi Freshwater mussel.

Kākaho Culm of the *toetoe* grass.

Kākahoroa *kākaho* (culm of the *toetoe* grass); *roa* (long). The original name for Whakatāne.

Kakanui Correctly, Kakaunui. *Kakau* (to swim, or the stalk of a plant); *nui* (many). Many plant stalks, or swimming or crossing a river.

Kākāpō Ground parrot.

Kākāpuaka *kākā* (native parrot); *puaka* (dry twigs or flowers).

Kakaramea A contraction of Kakara taramea. Scent made from gum extracted from the leaves of spear-grass. See under Karamea.

Kākāriki Parakeet.

Kākātahi *kākā* (native parrot); *tahi* (single). One kākā.

Kakepuku Correctly, and in full, Kakīpuku-o-Kahurere. *Kakī* (neck); *puku* (swollen). The name was given hundreds of years ago by Rakataura, partly after his wife Kahurere, and partly because of the shape of the hill near Te Awamutu. It is also said that the full name is Kakepuku-te-aroaro-o-Kahukeke.

Kakīroa *kakī* (neck); *roa* (long). The name of a Waitaha ancestor, or one of the crew of the Ārai-te-uru canoe.

Kā-Kōhaka-ruru-whenua In standard Māori the name would appear as Ngā-kōhanga-ruru-whenua. *Ngā* (the); *kōhanga* (nest); *ruru-whenua* (large owl, or morepork). The nests of the large owls. Some southern Māori digging for gold in the 1860s cooked and ate these owls, giving this name to what later became Moonlight Gully.

Kāmahi A native tree.

Kamaka Rock or stone.

Kapiti Island.

Kamautūrua The fastening of two bundles. The name of a chief of the Ārai-te-uru canoe was given to the Burnett Range.

Kamo To bubble up. Descriptive of the hot springs.

Kamokamo Winking. When the chief Porourangi was about to be murdered, winking was adopted as a signal for the attack.

Kanapa Shining.

Kaniere The act of sawing greenstone.

Kanohi Eye, or face.

Kā-pākihi-whakatekateka-a-Waitaha *kā*, or *ngā* (the); *pākihi* (open grass country); *whakatekateka* (to play with a dart); *a* (of); *Waitaha* (a tribe). The open grass country where the Waitaha people would have room to play the game of throwing darts. It is a very old name for the Canterbury Plains, and there is an inference that there was no room for such sport in the hills and gullies of Otago.

Kapiti Short for Ko-te-waewae-kapiti-o-Tara-raua-ko-Rangitāne, The place where the boundaries of Tara and Rangitāne divide.

Kaponga A tree-fern.

Kāpoupou-o-te-Rakihouia The posts of Rakihouia, the son of Rākaihaitū, who dug the southern lakes. Rakihouia made a number of eel weirs, and this very old name for the Canterbury coast was given because of the posts he planted in the rivers in order to make eel weirs.

Kapo-wairua *kapo* (snatching); *wairua* (soul). A place in Tom Bowling Bay where demons snatch at the spirits of the dead as they pass to the afterlife.

Kapuarangi *kapua* (cloud); *rangi* (sky). Cloudy sky.

Kāpuka A native tree.

Kapuka-tau-moha-ka Snaring pigeons with a string. A name which describes pigeon-hunting on the slopes of Mount Cargill.

Kā-puke-māeroero *kā*, or *ngā* (the); *puke* (hill); *māeroero* (wild men of the hills). The hills of the wild men. This was the Māori name for the foothills of the Southern Alps.

Hay bales in Canterbury, at the foot of the Southern Alps, Kā-puke-māeroero.

Kapuni An assembly. A place named by Turi of the Aotea canoe where he and his men camped by a river.

Karaka A native tree.

Karamea A shortened form of Kakara-taramea. *Kakara* (scent); *taramea* (spear-grass). The scent was made from the gum extracted from the leaves of the spear-grass. The kakara taramea made by the women of the Karamea district was highly valued, and Māori travelled long distances to barter food and greenstone for it.

Karamū A native shrub.

Karangahake *karanga* (to welcome); *hake* (hunchback). Loosely translated as a Meeting of the hunchbacks, a phrase which describes the cluster of low hills in the vicinity.

Ōwhāroa Falls, Karangahake Gorge.

Karangahape A shellfish. There is a story that a hill on the East Coast was called Karanga-na-Hape, because the chief Hape pursued a wounded moa up a hillside. He attacked it with his taiaha (weapon), but it kicked him, his leg was broken, and he rolled down the hill.

Karangarua *karanga* (to call); *rua* (two).

Karāpiro *karā* (stone); *piro* (stinking).

Karapiti To fasten, or place side by side.

Karatia Māori form of Galatia, a missionary settlement on the Whanganui River, originally called Hikurangi.

Karekare Surf.

Kāretu Sweet-scented grass.

Karioi To loiter. A place where the Māori sometimes lingered.

Kāriri Māori form of Galilee. Early mission station.

Karitāne *kari* (to dig); *tāne* (men). Men digging. This may be a reference to the digging of a ditch to catch eels. Another explanation is that while the Huriawa pā was being besieged, some of the men slipped out on a fishing expedition leaving only the wounded (kari) to defend the pā.

Karori In full, Te-kaha-o-ngā-rore, The rope of the snares. Before European settlement the Karori valley was noted for its birds.

Karoro The proper name is Kararoa. *Kara* (beach); *roa* (long). Long shelving beach.

Kartigi Correctly, Kātiki. *Kā*, or *ngā* (the); *tiki* (carved figure). The tiki.

Karu-moe-rangi To day dream.

Katikati Nibbling. In full, Katikati-o-Tama-te-kapua, The nibbling of Tama-te-kapua. When they reached this place, Tama-te-kapua's men ate their food quickly, but the captain of the Arawa canoe kept nibbling his, hence the name.

Katipō A small venomous spider.

Kauaeranga No crossing here.

Kauana Māori form of the name Cowan, who was an early settler in the Ōreti River basin.

Kau-ara-Paoa *kau* (to swim); *ara* (path); *Paoa (Pawa)*. The route by which Pawa swam across the river. Pawa was Kupe's servant. He went up the Whanganui River, and swam to the other side to get some kōrau (native turnip) and was drowned. This was an important place because

here Kupe heard voices. They were the voices of the weka, kōkako, and tīwaiwaka. When he found they were birds and not men, he returned to the mouth of the river.

Kaukapakapa *kau* (to swim); *kapakapa* (flapping). To swim with much splashing. There were wild ducks in the creek, and they were chased away or hunted with much flapping of their wings.

Kaukau Corrupt form of Kākā, a native parrot.

Kaungaroa Correctly, Kauangaroa. *Kauanga* (ford); *roa* (long). Long ford.

Kauri Short for Kauri-hohore, a bald or smooth-barrelled kauri tree.

Kauroa *kau* (to swim); *roa* (long). To swim for a long time.

Kauwae whakatoro *kauwae* (jaw); *whakatoro* (to stretch out). The Ngāi-Tahu tribe, fighting against Ngāti-māmoe, sent out decoys at Hillend. Then they closed round their victims like jaws round food.

Kawakawa A native tree. Kawakawa at East Cape is in full Te Kawakawa-mai-tawhiti, and has come from Hawaiki.

Kawarau *kawa* (shrub); *rau* (many). Many shrubs.

Kawarau Gorge, Central Otago.

Kawatiri There are many explanations of the meaning of the Māori name for the Buller River, some of which are lengthy. A noted authority believed that it should really have been Ko Awatere, The swift river.

Kawau Shag.

Kawerau *kawe* (to carry); *rau* (many). Many

carriers. The district was first settled by the Tini-o-Kawe-rau tribe from Hawaiki, which took its name from a chief.

The Buller River, Kawatiri.

Kāwhia In full, Ka-awhia. The name was given by Turi of the Aotea canoe when he entered the harbour. An awhiawhi was a ceremony performed on entering a new land to protect the explorers from evil influences. Each phrase of the karakia (chant) that Turi used began with ka.

Kawiti The Māori chief who fought against the British forces in the Bay of Islands.

Kēkerengū Black beetle. The name comes from a young Māori chief who had to flee to this place because of the enmity of Rangihaeata.

Kenana Māori form of Canaan.

Kenepuru Sandy silt.

Kerepehi Clod of earth. An old Māori said that it was a clod of earth 'easy to hold'.

Kerikeri To keep on digging.

Keteketerau *keteketeke* (to click the tongue); *rau* (many). Many clickings of the tongue. Tara, son of Whātonga, set out to avenge the killing of his dog. He landed at what was then the outlet of the Ahuriri lagoon, Napier, and jumped ashore. Then he remembered he had left his pūtātara (trumpet) at Wairoa, and gave vent to his surprise by many clickings of his tongue.

Ketemarae *kete* (kit); *marae* (courtyard). Basket on the marae. An old woman at the pā on the site of Normanby had only one basket of food to give to visitors. She put it on the marae.

Ketetahi *kete* (basket); *tahi* (one). One basket.

Kiekie A native vine.

Kihikihi Cicada. An onomatopoeic name.

Kikowhakarere *kiko* (body); *whakarere* (cast away). Bodies cast away. The Māori of Whangapoua surprised those at Kikowhakarere, but were defeated. They had to leave many behind who were dead or wounded, and from this the place received its name.

An aerial view of the Kerikeri basin.

Kilmog A whaler's pronunciation of *kirimoho* (a species of *mānuka*, or tea-tree). It was used to make an infusion of tea.

Kimiākau *kimi* (to look for); *ākau* (coast). To look for the coast. A band of explorers followed the course of the Arrow River to see if they could find a way through to the West Coast.

Kimihia To seek.

Kinohaku *kino* (bad, or ugly); *haku* (kingfish).

Kiokio A native fern.

Kiore Native rat.

Kioreroa *kiore* (rat); *roa* (long). Long rat.

Kirikau *kiri* (skin); *kau* (bare). Naked. A battle in which the contestants were naked was fought here long ago.

Kirikiri-katata *kirikiri* (a mass of rock); *katata* (sharp points). A sharp-pointed mass of rock. The Māori name for Mount Cook. See also Aorangi.

Kirikiriroa *kirikiri* (gravel); *roa* (long). Long stretches of gravel. The Māori name for Hamilton.

Kirikōpuni Dark-skinned eel.

Kiriohinekai The skin of Hinekai. It was a hot pool at Rotorua which was useful in the cure of skin diseases.

Kiripaka Quartz, or flint.

Kiritaki To pull off the bark. There was a tōtara tree from which a great deal of bark was taken.

Kiwi Native flightless bird.

Kiwitahi *kiwi* (bird); *tahi* (one). Single kiwi.

Kiwitea *kiwi* (bird); *tea* (white). White kiwi.

Kōhai A form of *kōwhai* (flowering tree).

Kōhanga Nest.

Kohekohe A native tree.

Kohi Seasick. When the Mataatua canoe paddled towards the shore in the Bay of Plenty, the ground-swell made Wairaka, the daughter of Toroa, sick.

Kohimārama *kohi* (point); *mārama* (light). Light on a headland.

Kōhua-ora Cooked in an earth oven while alive. It refers to an event of long ago at Papatoetoe.

Kohukete *kohu* (mist); *kete* (basket). Mist in the form of a basket. The chief Koha took this form of mist as the sign of an approaching enemy.

Kohukohu Moss, seaweed, a plant, or a tree.

Kohumaru *kohu* (mist); *maru* (sheltered). Sheltered from the fog.

Kohunui *kohu* (mist); *nui* (big). Big mist, or ground mist.

Kōhuratahi *kōhura* (to sprout); *tahi* (single).

Kohutai *kohu* (mist); *tai* (tide). Sea foam.

Kōiro Conger eel.

Kōkako Native crow.

Kōkakoriki *kōkako* (crow); *riki* (little, or few). Few kokako.

Kōkiri To dash forward, or charge.

Kokonga Angle or corner. The name probably comes from the bend in the river.

Kōkopu Small freshwater fish.

Kokori A small bay.

Kōkōwai Red earth, from which red ochre was obtained by burning.

Kōmata End of a range of hills.

Kongahu Boulders. There are many boulders in this part of the Buller district.

Kōnini Fruit of native fuchsia.

Kōpaki To wrap.

Kopi-o-kaitangata *kopi* (gorge); *o* (of); *kaitangata* (man-eater). Cannibal gorge. Parties of Māori travelled to the west coast through this gorge, their passage being marked by cannibal feasts. An alternative name is Kā-pai-ō-kaitangata, Good feed of human flesh.

Kōpū Belly.

Kōpua Deep pool.

Kōpuarahi *kōpua* (deep pool); *rahi* (large). Large deep hole.

Kōpuaranga *kōpua* (deep hole); *ranga* (shoal of fish). Fish in a deep pool.

Kōpuawhara *kōpua* (deep pool); *whara* (plant). Deep pool with astelia growing round it.

Kōpuku Closely woven cloak.

Kōpūreherehe *kōpū* (belly); *reherehe* (wrinkled). The name refers to eels which had been fat, but had become shrunken and wrinkled.

Kopuriki *kopu* (small fish); *riki* (few). Hardly any fish.

Kōpūriki *kōpū* (belly); *riki* (little). Little stomach.

Kopūtai High tide. Some Māori landed at Port Chalmers and went soundly to sleep. When they woke they found that their canoes had drifted away on the tide. They shouted 'Kopūtai!' ('High tide!')

Kōputaroa *kōputa* (snare for catching parakeets); *roa* (long). Long snare.

Koputauaki To relax comfortably after a feast, which was exactly what happened after a cannibal banquet.

Koputīraha Lying back with the arms above the head. An attitude adopted by a chief at this place, which is now the business centre of Nelson.

Kōrakonui *kōrako* (albino); *nui* (big). Big albino.

Koranui Short for Koro-koronui. *Korokoro* (throat); *nui* (big). Big throat. The valley is long and narrow and may be said to resemble a throat.

Koreke Quail.

Kōrere Channel.

Koriniti Māori form of Corinth. A missionary settlement on the Whanganui River.

Kōrito Unexpanded leaves, or a variety of greenstone.

Korokata Māori form of Golgotha. Te Rauparaha raided this place, just outside Whanganui, and fourteen years later the Reverend Richard Taylor was so horrified by the number of human bones to be seen there that he called the place Golgotha.

Korokoro Throat.

Koromiko Native veronica.

Kororāreka *kororā* (blue penguin); *reka* (sweet, or tasty). An old chief lay dying and expressed a wish for a penguin. After much searching one was found. When it was cooked he was too weak to eat it, but he drank some of the water in which it had been boiled, and murmured, 'Ka reka te kororā!' ('How sweet is the penguin!')

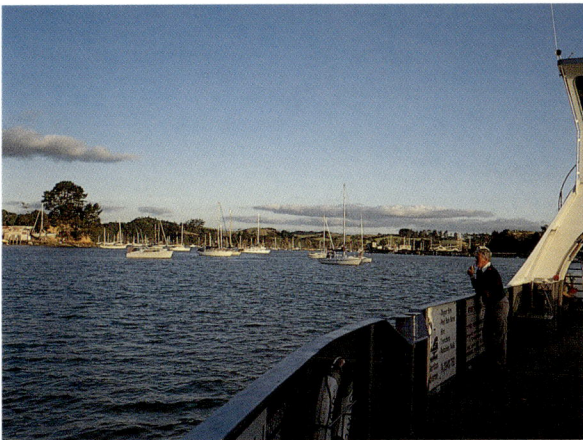

The Ōpua-Russell Ferry. Kororāreka is the Māori name for Russell.

Koru To fold, or folded.

Ko-te-kete-ika-a-Tutekawa The fish basket of Tutekawa. A proverb which applied to Lakes Forsyth and Ellesmere because they were so full of fish.

Kotemaori Incorrect form of Te Moari, The giant swing.

Kotinga Boundary line.

Kōtuku White heron. It is an abbreviation of the Māori name for Lake Brunner, Kōtuku-whakaoka. *Whakaoka* (to stab). The reference is to the kōtuku darting its long, sharp beak down to catch fish. Another name for Lake Brunner is Kōtuku-moana.

Koukou-parata Tame owl. Māori name for Port Levy.

Kōura Crayfish.

Kōurariki Whale-feed. Māori name for Cape Providence.

Koutu Promontory. A descriptive name.

Kōwai Shortened form of Kōwhai (flowering tree).

Kōwhai Flowering tree.

Kōwhatu Stone.

Kūaotuna *kūao* (young); *tuna* (eel). Young of eels.

Kuirau *kui* (old woman); *rau* (many). A picnic spot at Rotorua where the old women cooked the kai (food).

Kūmara Sweet potato. Kūmara on the West Coast, however, was named after a flower, of either the convolvulus or the bush-lawyer. It may originally have been kohi-mara.

Kumeroa *kume* (to pull); *roa* (long). A long pull.

Kumeū *kume* (to pull); *ū* (breast). Pulling the breasts. This is probably an action similar to that performed by Ruataupere of Ngāti-Porou. To incite a war party to avenge her cousin's death, she bared her bosom and pulled her breasts.

Kupenga-a-Kupe *kupenga* (net); *a* (of); *Kupe* (the famous explorer). Kupe left a net here at Jackson's Head as a sign of his having been there.

Kurīpuni *kurī* (native dog); *puni* (place of encampment).

Kurīwao *kurī* (dog); *wao* (bush). Wild dog.

Kurow Correctly, Kohurau. *Kohu* (mist); *rau* (many). Many fogs. The name probably came originally from one of the crew of the Ārai-te-uru.

Kūwhā-rua-o-Kahu As Kahu-mata-momoe went ashore at Lake Rotoiti, he threw off his clothes. His grandsons laughed and shouted, 'Ho! Ho! see, there go Kahu's legs!' and so the place was named.

M

Māeneene Smooth.

Maerewhenua Possibly this should be Maero-whenua. *Maero* (original inhabitants); *whenua* (land). Land of the wild men, or strange folk. An alternative meaning and spelling could be Maru-whenua; *maru* (shelter). The name is applied to the rock shelters with their unusual Māori paintings near Duntroon.

Maero Wild men.

Māhaki Mild, or calm.

Māhakipawa *māhaki* (calm); *pawa* (smoke). When Te Rauparaha raided the valley, the inhabitants saw him coming and set fire to their pā. Te Rauparaha saw the smoke rising calmly in the air, and said, 'I see smoke!'

Mahana Warm.

Māharahara To remember another's fault.

Mahau Shelter.

Maheno Island. The name was conferred by a Pākehā.

Māhēpuku A rounded sinker. The Māori name for Pepin Island.

Māhia To sound, or resound. The Māhia Peninsula was named Te Māhia-mai-Tawhiti after a place in Tahiti.

Māhinahina Refers to grey hair.

Māhinapua *Māhina* (proper name); *pua* (flower). Māhina's flower.

Mahitahi Correctly, Maitahi. *Mai* (garment); *tahi* (one). Single garment.

Māhoe A native tree.

Māhoenui *māhoe* (native tree); *nui* (big, or plenty of). Many māhoe trees.

Māhoetahi *māhoe* (native tree); *tahi* (single). Single māhoe tree.

Mahunui The name of the canoe in which Māui came to New Zealand. This canoe was the South Island, Te Waka-a-Māui, from which he fished up (discovered) Te Ika-a-Māui, the North Island. Also Maahunui.

Mahurangi One of the explanations of the name is that the Tainui canoe called in here before the portage over the Tamaki Isthmus, and that this place, later known as Warkworth, was so-called after the chieftainess who designed the Tainui canoe in Hawaiki.

Mahuta Named after the third Māori King, son of Tāwhiao.

Māia Brave.

Maiki The high place. The peak where the flagstaff stands at Russell.

Maimai The place in Westland is not named after a

Māori word, but comes from a corruption of the Australian word for a rough camp or bivouac, brought over by the gold-diggers.

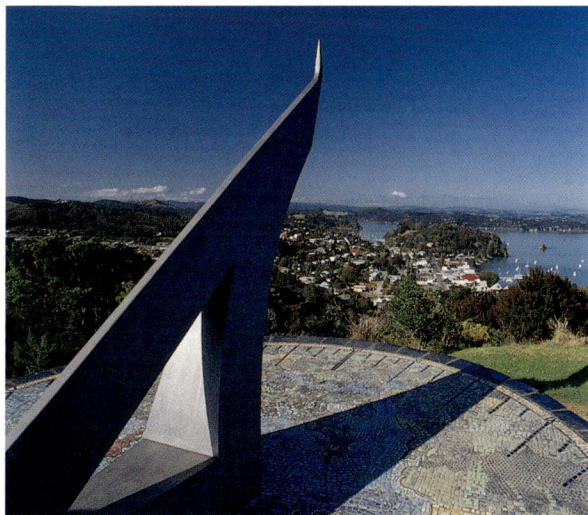

Flagstaff Hill or Maiki, at Russell.

Mairangi Shortened form of Ōmairangi, the place of Mairangi.

Maire-kura *maire* (native tree); *kura* (red garment). Red garment hanging on a maire tree. A chief dared his enemies to cross the Whanganui River by hanging his red garment in a tree.

Māīroa *māī* (mussels out of their shells); *roa* (many).

Maitai The proper spelling is Maitahi, and refers to one particular matai or mai (black pine) which grew on the bank of the river.

Mākāhu *mā* (white); *kāhu* (hawk). White hawk.

Mākara Head, or **Makara**, to come or go.

Mākaraka *mā* (short for *manga*: stream); *karaka* (native tree). A place where karaka trees grew by a stream.

Makarau *maka* (to throw); *rau* (to catch in a net).

Mākāretu *mā* (stream); *kāretu* (sweet-scented grass). Stream where the sweet-scented grass grows.

Makarewa *maka* (fish-hook); *rewa* (floating). Fish-hooks floating on the water. After baiting hooks to catch eels, the local Māori found them floating on the surface of the water after a storm.

Mākarini Named for Sir Donald McLean.

Makarora *maka* (South Island form of *manga*: stream); *rora* (spread out).

Makarore *maka* (part of a bird-snare); *rore* (to ensnare).

Mākatote *mā* (stream); *katote* (tree-fern). Tree-ferns growing by a stream.

Mākauri *mā* (stream); *kauri* (native tree). Kauri growing by a stream.

Mākawhio *mā* (stream); *whio* (blue duck). Stream of the blue duck.

Mākerikeri *mā* (stream); *kerikeri* (rushing violently). Turbulent stream.

Makerōnia Māori form of Macedonia. The pā was built at the time of the Hauhau wars.

Maketū Named after a place in Hawaiki.

Mākiekie *mā* (stream); *kiekie* (native flower plant). Stream where the kiekie grows.

Mākikihi *mā* (stream); *kikihi* (cicada). Stream of the cicadas. Or kikihi may refer to the sound of the cicadas, in which case the meaning is Murmuring stream.

Mākino *mā* (stream); *kino* (bad).

Mākirikiri *mā* (stream); *kirikiri* (gravelly). Gravelly stream.

Mākōhine *mā* (stream); *kōhine* (girl). Girl's stream.

Mākōtuku *mā* (stream); *kōtuku* (white heron). Stream of the white heron. Alternatively, *kōtuku* could be *kōtukutuku* (fuchsia).

Mākōura *mā* (stream); *kōura* (freshwater crayfish 'crawlies'). Crayfish stream.

Mākōwhai *mā* (stream); *kōwhai* (native tree). Kōwhai stream. A name given by a Pākehā.

Mākū Wet.

Mākurī *mā* (stream); *kurī* (dog). Dog creek.

Mamaku Tree-fern.

Mana Power. Mana Island near Wellington is, in full, Te Mana-o-Kupe-ki-Aotea-roa, the ability of Kupe to cross the ocean to Aotearoa. It was Kupe's daughter who suggested that the name be given to the island.

Manaia A carved Māori figure with a beak. Manaia in Taranaki was named after a local Māori chief. Manaia on the south side of Whangarei Harbour was named after a chief who climbed the hill.

When at the summit he quarrelled with his wife and kicked her and his slave, and the whole family were turned into stones by the gods.

Manakau *mana* (authority or prestige); *kau* (alone). Prestige alone. Te Rauparaha subdued the local inhabitants by means of his prestige without having to resort to war.

Manapōuri Short for Manawa-popore. *Manawa* (heart); *popore* (throbbing). Anxious heart, a name given by a traveller whose canoe was threatened by a storm. The true name of the lake is Moturau, meaning Many islands.

Lake Manapōuri.

Manaroa *mana* (power); *roa* (long).

Manawaora *manawa* (heart); *ora* (healthy).

Manawarū Anxious, apprehensive, or enraptured.

Manawa-tahi Out of breath. The name of the Three Kings Islands. The chief Raura owned one of them and swam across from the mainland, arriving exhausted on the shore of the island.

Manawatū Heart standing still with fear, or depressed spirit. Haunui was pursuing his wife, and when he came to the river he held his hand to his heart and gave it the name Manawatū.

Manga-a-te-tipua *manga* (stream); *a* (of); *te* (the); *tipua* (demon). Goblin creek, a suitable name for the boiling stream at Ketetahi.

Mangahao Short for Manga-ā-hao. *Manga* (stream);

ā (of); *hao* (netting). Stream where cockabullies are caught.

Mangaharakeke *manga* (stream); *harakeke* (flax). Flax creek.

Mangahoe *manga* (stream); *hoe* (to paddle). Paddling in the stream.

Mangahuia *manga* (stream); *huia* (extinct bird). Huia stream.

Mangaiti *manga* (stream); *iti* (small). Little stream.

Mangakāhia *manga* (stream); *kāhia*, or *kōhia* (passion vine). Passion vine stream.

Mangakaiwhiria *manga* (stream); *kaiwhiria* (climbing plant).

Mangakino *manga* (stream); *kino* (bad). Useless stream.

Mangakura *manga* (stream); *kura* (red, or red ochre). Red stream.

Mangamāhoe *manga* (stream); *māhoe* (whitewood tree). Māhoe stream.

Mangamāhū *manga* (stream); *māhū* (gentle). Gently flowing stream.

Mangamaire *manga* (stream); *maire* (tree, New Zealand olive). Maire stream.

Mangamako Probably short for Mangamakomako. *Manga* (stream); *makomako* (wineberry tree). Wineberry stream.

Mangamate *manga* (stream); *mate* (death). Stream of death.

Mangāmāunu *mangā* (barracouta fish); *māunu* (bait). Barracouta bait.

Mangamingi Probably Mangamingimingi in full. *Manga* (stream); *mingimingi* (shrub). Mingimingi stream.

Mangamuka *manga* (stream); *muka* (shoot of *nīkau*). Nīkau palm stream.

Mangamutu *manga* (stream); *mutu* (finished). Dead-end stream.

Mangangārara *manga* (stream); *ngārara* (lizard). Lizard stream.

Māngangūkaiota *manga* (scraps); *ngū* (eat greedily); *kai* (food); *ota* (raw). I will eat you raw. Said by one chief to another if he dared to cross a line between them. The chief did so, and was eaten raw.

Manganui *manga* (stream); *nui* (big). Big stream.

Manganuiateao *manga* (stream); *nui* (big); *a* (of); *te* (the); *ao* (world). The great stream of the land. It is famous in legend, and has two other names equally grand: The powerful and famous river of Rongomai, and The river of ever-dancing waters and steep, echoing cliffs.

Mangaohae *manga* (stream); *o* (of); *Hae* (proper name). The stream of Hae.

Mangaohutu *manga* (stream); *o* (of); *Hutu* (proper name). The stream of Hutu.

Mangaone *manga* (stream); *one* (beach). Sandy stream.

Mangaonoho *manga* (stream); *o* (of); *Noho* (proper name). Noho's stream.

Mangaoranga Correctly, Manga-o-Rongomai. *Manga* (stream); *o* (of); *Rongomai* (a god). Stream of Rongomai.

Mangaotaki *manga* (stream); *o* (of); *Taki* (proper name). Taki's stream.

Mangaowera *manga* (stream); *o* (of); *Wera* (proper name). Wera's stream.

Mangapai *manga* (stream); *pai* (good). Stream of good water.

Mangapākehā The correct name is Mangapākia. *Manga* (stream); *pākia* (to be touched).

Mangapākihi *manga* (stream); *pākihi* (open grass country). Grassy stream.

Mangapapa *manga* (stream); *papa* (flat country). Stream through flat country.

Mangapēhi *manga* (stream); *pēhi* (sticks for making fire, or trouble). Stream of trouble.

Mangapiko *manga* (stream); *piko* (bent). Crooked stream.

Mangapiri *manga* (stream); *piri* (to hide, or native burr). Hidden stream.

Mangapōuri *manga* (stream); *pōuri* (dark). Dark stream.

Mangapuaka *manga* (stream); *puaka* (bird-snare). Stream of the bird-snare.

Mangapūrua *manga* (stream); *pūrua* (abundant, or plenty). Stream of plenty.

Mangarākau *manga* (stream); *rākau* (tree or timber). Stream by the trees.

Mangaramarama *manga* (stream); *ramarama* (myrtle tree).

Mangarātā *manga* (stream); *rātā* (tree). Rātā stream.

Mangarawa *manga* (stream); *rawa* (swamp). Swampy stream.

Mangarengarenga *manga* (stream); *rengarenga* (renga lily). Stream of lilies.

Mangareporepo *manga* (stream); *reporepo* (soft mud). Muddy creek.

Mangarimu *manga* (stream); *rimu* (tree). Rimu stream.

Mangaroa *manga* (stream); *roa* (long). Long stream.

Mangarōhutu *manga* (stream); *rōhutu* (myrtle). Myrtle stream.

Mangarua *manga* (stream); *rua* (two). Two streams.

Mangatainoka *manga* (stream); *tainoka* (native broom). Broom stream.

Mangatangi *manga* (stream); *tangi* (weeping). Babbling brook.

Mangatapu *manga* (stream); *tapu* (sacred). Forbidden stream.

Mangatarata *manga* (stream); *tarata* (tree). Tarata stream.

Mangatāwhiri *manga* (stream); *tāwhiri* (tree). Stream where the tāwhiri grows.

Mangatea *manga* (stream); *tea* (clear, or white). Clear stream.

Mangaterā *manga* (stream); *te* (the); *rā* (sun). Sunny stream.

Mangatere *manga* (stream); *tere* (to flow). Flowing stream.

Mangateretere *manga* (stream); *teretere* (swiftly flowing). Swift-flowing stream.

Mangatina *manga* (stream); *tina* (exhausted). The first Māori to reach the stream were exhausted by the effort of crossing.

Mangatini *manga* (stream); *tini* (many). Stream with many branches. The country this stream in the Buller district flows through is very broken.

Mangatītī *manga* (stream); *tītī* (mutton-bird). Stream of the mutton-birds.

Mangatoetoe *manga* (stream); *toetoe* (plume grass). Toetoe stream.

Mangatoki Possibly a contraction of Mangatītoki. *Manga* (stream); *tītoki* (tree). Tītoki stream.

Māngatu *mā* (stream); *ngatu* (part of the *raupō*). Stream of the reeds.

Mangawai *manga* (stream); *wai* (water).

Mangawara *manga* (stream); *wara* (indistinct sound).

Mangaweka *manga* (stream); *weka* (wood-hen). Creek of the wood-hens.

Mangawhai *manga* (stream); *Whai* (name of a chief). Te Whai fled from the Ngāpuhi and settled on the headland where the rivers meet. The name means River of Te Whai.

Mangawharariki *manga* (stream); *wharariki* (a kind of flax). Stream where the flax grows.

Mangawharawhara *manga* (stream); *wharawhara* (perching lily). Wharawhara stream.

Mangawhare *manga* (stream); *whare* (house). Stream by the house.

Mangawhata *manga* (stream); *whata* (raised storehouse). Stream by the storehouse.

Mangawhero *manga* (stream); *whero* (red). Red stream.

Māngere Lazy. When Ihenga crossed the Waikato, he came to this place and rested while his young men prepared food. They took so long that he was angry, and named the place Laziness.

Mangōnui *mangō* (shark); *nui* (big). Large shark.

Mangōparerua Two hammerhead sharks.

Mangōrei *mangō* (shark); *rei* (tooth). Shark's tooth.

Mangungu Closely knit, or woven.

Māniatoto The name in full is Māniaototo. *Mānia* (plain); *o* (of); *toto* (blood). It was the scene of many bloody battles.

Māniatutu *mānia* (plain); *tutu* (tree). Plain where the tutu grows.

Manuherekia *manu* (bird); *herekia* (tied). The tied bird. A Māori scout tied a wounded *kākā* here to mark the crossing place.

Mānuka Tea-tree.

Manukau *manu* (bird); *kau* (to wade). Wading birds. The original name of the Manukau Harbour was Mānuka (tea-tree). It may have received this name when Kahu-mata-momoe set up a mānuka post there as a rāhui or sacred mark. On the other hand, it is likely that the name is of even greater antiquity. There is an old proverb which says, Kei te tua o Mānuka, tē kite muri ki te kupenga-o-Taramainuku (When you pass out beyond the Mānuka waters, do not look back until you reach, or pass, the fishing net of Tara).

Manunui Correctly, Mananui. *Mana* (prestige); *nui* (large). Great prestige. It refers to the power and prestige of the chief Paparangi.

Manupīrua Two little birds.

Manurewa *manu* (kite); *rewa* (floating). Floating kite. A kite once broke loose at Ōnehunga and floated over Manurewa.

Manutahi *manu* (bird); *tahi* (single). Solitary bird.

Manutītī *manu* (bird); *tītī* (mutton-bird). The small island in Dusky Sound was so named because there was a colony of birds there, and the Māori could always collect a few in the autumn.

Manutuke *manu* (bird); *tuke* (elbow, or to twitch).

Manuwhaea *manu* (bird); *whaea* (split). The split bird.

Māori Native to the country. When the word Māori enters into a name, as in Māori Hill, Māori Creek, etc., it is safe to say that it has been conferred by a Pākehā.

Māpere To fly.

Māpiu In full, Māpiupiu. *Mā* (stream); *piupiu* (fern). Ferny creek.

Māpou Native tree.

Māpourika The word is unknown. It may possibly be a South Island form of Mapouriki.

Māpouriki *māpou* (tree); *riki* (little). The small māpou trees.

Māpua Bearing an abundance of fruit.

Maraekākaho *marae* (village assembly ground); *kākaho* (plumes of the *toetoe*). The courtyard surrounded by plume grass.

Maraekura *marae* (courtyard); *kura* (man of prowess). When Turi reached the Kaupoko-nui River his enchanted cloak opened twice and spread out, and he called the place Maraekura.

Maraeroa *marae* (courtyard); *roa* (long). Long plaza.

Maraetai *marae* (open space); *tai* (coast). Open space by the seashore.

Maraetui *marae* (open space); *tui* (sea). Flat area at the head of the bay.

Maraeweka *marae* (courtyard); *weka* (wood-hen). Weka on the marae.

Mārahau *māra* (garden); *hau* (wind). Windy garden.

Marakeke Probably Mārakerake (bald).

Marama Moon.

Maramarua *marama* (month); *rua* (two). Two months.

Marangai East wind.

Maranui The name in full should be Maraenui. *Marae* (expanse); *nui* (big). Great expanse. It refers to the expanse of ocean visible from Lyall Bay.

Māraroa *māra* (cultivation); *roa* (long). Long cultivated area.

Mārarua *māra* (cultivation); *rua* (two). Two plantations.

Mārawhiupungarehu *māra* (cultivation); *whiu* (to throw); *pungarehu* (ashes). The cultivation overcast with ashes.

Mareretu The original name has been contracted. *Marere* (to let down); *retu* (part of a fishing net). To let down the net.

Marewa Raised up, or light soil.

Marino Calm, or peaceful.

Māriri Unripe fruit of the tawa tree.

Marokopa *maro* (kilt, or stiff); *kopa* (to fold, or lame). The place where Turi of the Aotea canoe folded his girdle, or where he went lame.

Maromākū *maro* (girdle); *mākū* (wet). Wet kilt.

Maropiu *maro* (kilt); *piu* (to swing). Kilt waving in the breeze.

Marotiri *maro* (apron); *tiri* (to throw or place beside). Placed beside the apron.

Mārua Valley.

Māruakoa *mārua* (valley); *koa* (glad). Happy valley.

Maruia Sheltered, like a valley deep in the hills.

Matā Quartz or flint.

Matahara *mata* (face); *hara* (ugly). Ugly face.

Matahiwi *mata* (face); *hiwi* (ridge). The ridge above the cliff.

Matahorua *mata* (face, or eye); *horua* (sobbing). Weeping.

Mātai Sea, or **Matai**, a native tree.

Mataīhuka Black pine.

Mataīnui *mataī* (black pine); *nui* (big, or many). Plenty of black pine.

Mātairangi An observation post on a hill, so named because of its commanding position on Tinakori Hill.

Mātaitakiara *mātai* (look-out point); *takiara* (morning star). The look-out point from which the morning star can be seen.

Mātaiwhetū *mātai* (to look at); *whetū* (star). To gaze at the stars.

Matakana Distrustful, or wary.

Matakānui *mata* (face); *kā* (blow, or scar); *nui* (big). The scarred face of a big cliff.

Matakinokino *mata* (face); *kinokino* (ugly). Ill-favoured face.

Mātakitaki To gaze at. The name was given to a number of places that Kupe and others inspected when they first came to New Zealand.

Matakohe *mata* (headland); *kohe* short for *kohekohe* (a tree). Pinnacle of land where kohekohe trees grow.

Matamata Point, or extremity. The point of land on which the pā (fortified village) was built projected like a tongue into the surrounding swamp.

Mātāmau Stingy. Or *mātā* (heap); *mau* (products of the soil). Heap of vegetables.

Matanehunehu *mata* (headland); *nehunehu* (spray). A headland drenched with flying spray. In a stiff northerly the spray flies right over the cliff.

Matangi Breeze.

Matangirau *matangi* (breeze); *rau* (leaf). Wind among the leaves.

Matanuku *mata* (cliff); *nuku* (to move or extend). Kahu-mata-momoe came to a cliff where there was a stone projecting from the face, and he named it for this reason.

Matapehi-o-te-rangi The first streak of dawn from the heavens. Māori name for McLaren's Peak, Nelson.

Matapīa *mata* (headland); *pīa* (to bathe with water). Headland washed by the sea.

Matapōuri Gloomy, a black teal, or a shellfish.

Mātapu To make clear of tapu. There was a prolific miro tree at this place which attracted flocks of pigeons. An old chief made it tapu or sacred to himself so that all the pigeons would be his. No doubt it became necessary to clear the tree of tapu at a later date if others were to have a share of the pigeons.

Mātārae A headland.

Matarau A number of points, used in describing a rocky shore.

Matarawa *mata* (headland); *rawa* (numerous). Many headlands.

Matariki The Pleiades, or the north-east sea-breeze.

Mataroa *mata* (headland); *roa* (long). Long headland.

Matata Dividing waters.

Matatapu *mata* (headland); *tapu* (sacred). Sacred headland.

Mātauri Bay, Northland.

Matātoki *matā* (flint); *toki* (adze). Flint adze.

Matau Fish-hook. At one place this name was given to a river which has a bend resembling a fish-hook, to another where there is a beach of the same shape. Matau, the original name for the Clutha River, was properly Mata-au, a current or eddy in an expanse of water.

Matauira *mata* (point of land); *uira* (lightning, or gleaming).

Mataura Reddish, eddying water. The swamp water which drains into the river is impregnated with iron oxide.

Mātauri *mā* (stream); *tauri* (ornament of feathers).

Mātāwai Fountain head, or source of a spring.

Matawhāura Warfare.

Matawhero *mata* (face); *whero* (red). Red face.

Matiaha After Matiaha Tira Mōrehu.

Mātiere *mā* (stream); *tiere* (scent). Scented stream.

Matiu Somes Island in Wellington Harbour was named after Matiu, the daughter of Kupe.

Mātukituki *mā* (stream); *tukituki* (dashing). The dashing or pounding stream. The Mātukituki River was probably named after a chief.

Matuku Bittern, or blue heron.

Mauku Small ground-ferns.

Maungaatua *maunga* (mountain); *atua* (god). Mountain of the gods.

Maungaharuru *maunga* (mountain); *haruru* (rumbling). Rumbling mountain. When the Tākitimu canoe was travelling down the East Coast on its way to search for greenstone, a high inland range was seen. The tohunga (priest) took a piece of wood, which received life and flew to the top of the range in the shape of a bird. The mountain gave forth a rumbling sound.

Maungakiekie, Cornwall Park, Auckland.

Maungahaumi *maunga* (mountain); *haumi* (piece of wood used to lengthen a canoe). When at Whakatāne, Pawa the captain sent a party of men ashore to get a suitable piece of timber for a topside plank for the canoe, and they found it on this mountain.

Maungahuka *maunga* (mountain); *huka* (snow). Snowy mountain. This peak in the Tararua Range was usually snow-covered.

Maungahura *maunga* (mountain); *hura* (bare). Bald mountain.

Maungakaramea *maunga* (mountain); *karamea* (red ochre). There are many colours in the mountain, which is known to Pākehā as Rainbow Mountain.

Maungakiekie *maunga* (mountain); *kiekie* (plant). The mountain where the kiekie grows abundantly. It is the Māori name for One Tree Hill in Auckland.

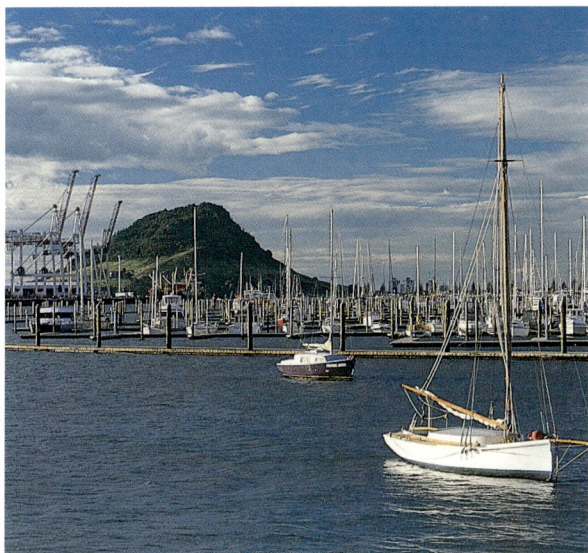

Mount Maunganui.

Maunganamu *maunga* (mountain); *namu* (sandfly). Sandfly mountain.

Maunganui *maunga* (mountain); *nui* (big). Large mountain.

Maungapōhatu *maunga* (mountain); *pōhatu* (rock). Rocky mountain.

Maungaraki *maunga* (mountain); *raki* (north). Mountains running in a northerly direction.

Maungataniwha *maunga* (mountain); *taniwha* (water monster). Taniwha mountain. Māori name for Mount Camel.

Maungatapere *maunga* (mountain); *tapere* (place for meeting). Meeting place of mountains.

Maungatapu *maunga* (mountain); *tapu* (sacred or forbidden). Forbidden mountain.

Maungatautari *maunga* (mountain); *tautari* (upright stick). Maungatautari was the ancient name for Cambridge.

Maungatī *maunga* (mountain); *tī* (cabbage tree). Cabbage tree mountain.

Maungatiki *maunga* (mountain); *tiki* (fungus). Mountain where the fungus grows.

Maungatua Correctly, Maungaatua. *Maunga* (mountain); *atua* (god or spirit). Mountain of the spirits.

Maungatūroto *maunga* (mountain); *tū* (to stand); *roto* (lake). Mountain standing in a lake. Several of the volcanic peaks in North Auckland are surrounded by swamps, which were originally lagoons.

Maungawera *maunga* (mountain); *wera* (hot, or burnt). Burnt mountain.

Maungawhau *maunga* (mountain); *whau* (native tree). Whau hill.

Mā-waro *mā* (stream); *waro* (charcoal). Charcoal stream.

Mawhera Widespread river mouth. It refers to the broad mouth of the Grey River, and is the site of Greymouth.

Mawheraiti Little Mawhera, a tributary of the Mawhera or Grey River.

Meremere Evening star.

Meretoto *mere* (greenstone club); *toto* (blood). Blood-drinking club. It is the Māori name for Ship Cove.

Mihamihanui *mihamiha* (to begin to grow); *nui* (large). A large patch of growing vegetation.

Mihiwaka *mihi* (to greet); *waka* (canoe). To greet the canoe. It is said that while the Mihiwaka tunnel was being constructed, a store had been kept by a Mrs Walker. The Māori labourers gave the Māori pronunciation to her name, and Mrs Walker became Mihiwaka.

Miki A ridge of hills. Named after a woman who was carried away by the māeroero, or wild men.

Mikimiki Surprised expression. It is said that the full name is Mimikitanga-o-te-mata-o-Ngatuere, The surprised look on the face of Ngatuere. The Wairarapa was being invaded by a force of Hauhau, who were met unexpectedly by the chief Ngatuere Tāwhirimātea Tāwhao, who had a surprised look on his face when he saw them.

Miko Young shoot of the nīkau palm.

Mimi Stream, or creek.

Mimihau Passing shower.

Mina To desire.

Minarapa *mina* (to desire); *rapa* (to seek for). To look for something earnestly desired. The stream on Mount Egmont/Taranaki was named after Minarapa, who accompanied Bell and Carrington when they climbed the mountain.

Mirowharerā *miro* (native tree); *whare* (house); *rā* (sun). The miro tree which shades the house from the sun. The name appears on early maps as Merofafara, and it has been suggested that it was a Māori attempt to pronounce Meadowbank, as there was a gum-diggers' settlement of that name in the locality at Waipoua Forest.

Mitimiti Shallow water.

Mititai *miti* (to lap); *tai* (the coast). To lap the coast. Insects flew so close to the water here that they seemed to lick it.

The boulders at Moeraki.

Moa Large, extinct, flightless bird. Most places such as Moa Flat, Moa Creek, Moa Point, etc. have been so-named because of the large number of moa bones found in the vicinity.

Moana Ocean, or large lake.

Moana-kōtuku *moana* (large lake); *kōtuku* (white heron). Lake of the white heron. Māori name for Lake Brunner where the kōtuku would often be seen.

Moana-nui-a-Kiwa *moana* (ocean); *nui* (big); *a* (of); *Kiwa* (an ocean god). The great ocean of Kiwa. The Pacific Ocean.

Moanataiari *moana* (ocean); *taiari* (dashing). The stormy ocean.

Moanawhenua-pōuri *moana* (ocean); *whenua* (land); *pōuri* (sad, or dark). Sombre sound, the Māori name for Edwardson Arm in Fiordland, notable because there was usually a cloud over it casting a dark shadow.

Moawhango *moa* (large extinct bird); *whango* (hoarse). Wheezy moa. Whango may be a corruption of whanga (valley), thus giving Moa valley.

Moeawatea *moe* (to sleep); *awatea* (daylight). Sleeping in the daytime.

Moehau *moe* (to sleep); *hau* (wind). Windy sleeping place. The name in full is Moehau-o-Tama-te-kapua. Tama-te-kapua, captain of the Arawa canoe, was buried at Cape Colville, and the name was given by his son Kahu-mata-momoe. Hau probably refers to the life essence, and the name means The sleeping sacredness of Tama-te-kapua. It may also mean The wind resting, or sleeping.

Moengawahine *moenga* (bed); *wahine* (woman). Woman's bed.

Moerā *moe* (to sleep); *rā* (the sun). Sleeping in the sun.

Moeraki *moe* (to sleep); *raki* (South Island form of *rangi*: sky, or day). A place for sleep by day.

Moerangi *moe* (to sleep); *rangi* (sky). Sleepy sky.

Moerewa *moe* (to sleep); *rewa* (floating like a bird apparently asleep). To sleep on high.

Moeroa *moe* (to sleep); *roa* (long). Long sleep, or resting, or sleeping place.

Moetapu *moe* (to sleep); *tapu* (sacred). Sacred sleep.

Moetere *moe* (to sleep); *tere* (swift). Swift sleep. Named after Moetere, who died in a snowstorm here on the Huiarau Range.

Mōhaka *mō* (used for); *haka* (dance). Place used for a dance. The name was imported from Hawaiki.

Mōhakatino *mō* (used); *haka* (dance); *tino* (exact,

precise). The river was named because Turi of the Aotea canoe departed in person (tino) after having slept at Mōkau.

Mōioio The little blue penguin.

Mōkai Captive.

Motuhora, or Whale Island, lies off the coast of Whakatāne.

Mōkau Sleeping place. Named by Turi because he slept there.

Mōkauiti Little Mōkau.

Mōkihinui *mōkihi* (raft of dry flax stalks); *nui* (big). Large raft.

Moko hīnau *moko* (lizard); *hīnau* (native tree).

Mokoia Tattooed. On Mokoia Island, Lake Rotorua, a chief was fatally stabbed over the eye in a closely tattooed place with a sharpened kō (digging implement), and the name is a pun: *moko* (tattoo); *kō* (digging implement). On the other hand, Mokoia, which was the original name for Panmure, was Mokoika, named after the taniwha (water monster) Mokoikahikuwaru, the lizard with eight tails.

Mōmona Good, fertile land.

Momorangi *momo* (offspring); *rangi* (the sky). Offspring of heaven.

Monowai The proper name is Manokīwai. *Mano* (a fixed channel); *kī* (full); *wai* (water). Channel full of water. It is a long narrow lake which is always full, although it receives no big streams or rivers. Monowai was as close as James McKerrow, the Pākehā discoverer, could get to the Māori name.

Mōrere A swing, or 'giant stride'.

Mororimu *moro* (wave); *rimu* (bull kelp). Kelp floating on the waves. A Māori chief who raided the pā reported his success by saying, 'Nothing now moves at Waipapa but the kelp in the sea.'

Motatau Correctly, Mōtautau, talking to oneself. In this place Ihenga was heard talking to himself.

Mōtītī Named after a place in Hawaiki because there was no firewood there. There is a proverb which concerns the Arawa canoe: Kei Mōtītī koe e noho ana: I suppose you are at Mōtītī, as you can find no firewood. Literally, extirpated.

Motu Island, or isolated clump of trees.

Motuara *motu* (island); *ara* (path). Island in the path of the canoe.

Motu-arohia *motu* (island); *arohia* (reconnoitred). The island that was spied upon.

Motueka In full, Motuweka. *Motu* (clump of trees); *weka* (wood-hen). Wood-hens in a grove of trees. The name originally came from Hawaiki, where it may have a different connotation. It is sometimes said to mean The crippled wood-hen — one which was kept as a lure to capture weka.

Motuhora Whale island. This is the name given to it by Pākehā, in which case it should be Motutohorā. It could also mean *motu* (clumps of trees); *hora* (scattered). Scattered patches of bush.

Motuihe *motu* (island); *Ihe* (short for Ihenga). The island was named after his nephew Ihenga by his uncle Kahu-mata-momoe.

Motukanae *motu* (island); *kanae* (mullet). Mullet island.

Motukaraka *motu* (island); *karaka* (native tree). Island of the karaka trees.

Motukārara *motu* (island); *kārara* (South Island form of *ngārara*: lizard). Lizard island.

Motukauatiiti *motu* (grove of trees); *kauati* (rubbing sticks to make fire); *iti* (little). Little fire-making tree grove. This was Corsair Bay, and Motukauatirahi (rahi meaning large) was Cass Bay. Both bays were noted for their groves of kaikōmako trees, the timber of which is specially suitable for fire-making.

Motukauatirahi See under Motukauatiiti.

Motukauri *motu* (island); *kauri* (native tree). Kauri island. The small island in the Hokianga River was covered with kauri.

Motukiekie *motu* (island); *kiekie* (plant). This is the Māori name for Stop Island in Dusky Sound. It is one of the few places in the sound where the kiekie grows.

Motukina *motu* (island); *kina* (sea-egg). The island of sea-eggs.

Motukiore *motu* (island); *kiore* (rat). Rat island. The island at the mouth of the Motueka River was infested by rats, and had to be abandoned for cultivation.

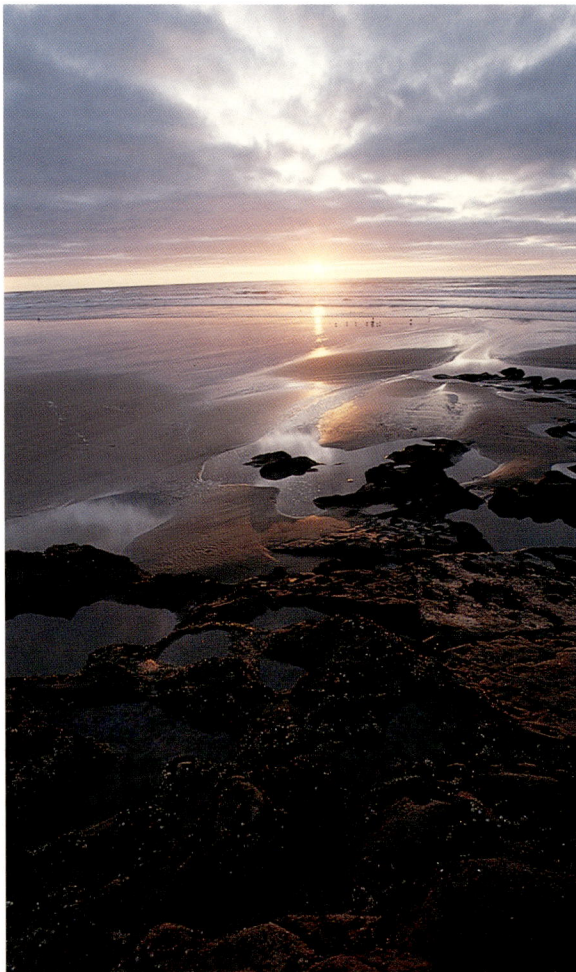

Muriwai beach, near Auckland.

Motunau *motu* (island); *nau* (scurvy grass). The grass grew here until it was eaten off by cattle.

Motungārara *motu* (island); *ngārara* (lizard). Lizard island.

Motunui *motu* (island); *nui* (big). Big island.

Motupiko *motu* (clump of trees); *piko* (winding, or curved). Straggling clumps of trees.

Motupipi *motu* (island); *pipi* (shellfish). Pipi island.

Motupiu *motu* (island); *piu* (to swing). Swinging island. This is Dog Island near Bluff. The story is that a southern tribe found a huge piece of greenstone in the sea. They drove it round to Bluff by following it in three canoes. It nearly eluded them several times and finally came to rest, where it remained as an island.

Motupōua *motu* (island); *pōua* (old man). Old man island. An old chief was buried on the summit of the hill.

Moturātā *motu* (island); *rātā* (native tree). Rātā island. Whale Island at Taieri Mouth and other places of this name were often bright with the scarlet blossoms of the rātā.

Moturau *motu* (island); *rau* (many, or a hundred). A hundred islands. The correct name for Lake Manapōuri.

Moturoa *motu* (island); *roa* (long, or tall). Long island. There are many places with this name. Moturoa is the largest of the islands in the Bay of Islands, whereas Moturoa in Queen Charlotte Sound is small, and there probably means Tall island.

Moturua *motu* (island); *rua* (two, or a pit). Two islands, Island with a pit.

Motutaiko *motu* (island); *taiko* (mutton-bird). Mutton-bird island.

Motutapu *motu* (island); *tapu* (sacred, or forbidden). Forbidden island.

Motutara *motu* (island); *tara* (gull). Gull island. Motutara Island in Lake Rotorua is frequented by the tarā-punga, the little lake gull.

Motutawa *motu* (island); *tawa* (native tree). Tawa island.

Motu-tawaki *motu* (island); *tawaki* (big or crested penguin). Penguin island. Māori name for Passage Island.

Motutere *motu* (island); *tere* (floating). Floating island. The name is found in several places; among others it is the Māori name for Castle

Rock at Coromandel, which looks like an island floating in the sky when it is surrounded by mist.

Motutīeke *motu* (island); *tīeke* (saddleback bird). Saddleback island.

Motutohorā See Motuhora.

Mourea Remnant. A name that comes from the Society Group.

Moutapu *mou* (fixed); *tapu* (sacred). On this island in the Grey River the Māori placed the bones of their dead in the branches of kahikatea, thus making them *tapu*.

Moutere Island.

Moutua In full Motutoa. *Motu* (island); *toa* (warrior). An island where warriors fought.

Muri-aroha-o-Kahu *muri* (breeze); *aroha* (affection); *o* (of); *Kahu* (Kahu-mata-momoe). Kahu-mata-momoe came to a dividing of the river Waihou and rested. As he felt the soft breeze, words of affection came to his lips.

Murihiku *muri* (end); *hiku* (tail). End of the tail. So named because it is the southern end of the South Island.

Muritai *muri* (breeze); *tai* (tide). Sea breeze.

Muriwai *muri* (end); *wai* (water). Backwater, or the junction of streams.

Muriwhenua *muri* (end); *whenua* (land). End of the land. Land's end. Māori name for North Cape.

Murupara *muru* (to wipe off); *para* (mud). To wipe off the mud.

N

Naenae Sandfly.

Namu Sandfly.

Naumai Come!

Nehutai Sea spray.

Ngaere Swamp

Ngāhape *ngā* (the); *hape* (hunchback, or cripple). The cripples.

Ngāhere The forest.

Ngāhinepōuri *ngā* (the); *hine* (women); *pōuri* (sad). The sorrowing women.

Ngaio A native tree.

Ngaionui *ngaio* (native tree); *nui* (big). The big ngaio.

Ngā-karikari-a-Rākaihautū *ngā* (the); *karikari* (excavations); *a* (of); *Rākaihautū* (South Island giant). The diggings of Rākaihautū. The great series of cold lakes in the South Island which were supposed to have been dug by Rākaihautū.

Ngākawau The shags.

Ngā-kurī-hine-poupou *ngā* (the); *kurī* (dog); *hine* (girl); *poupou* (plunged in). The dogs of the girl who plunged in.

Ngākuta Edible seaweed which was found at these bays.

Ngā-makawe-o-Maahu *ngā* (the); *makawe* (hair); *o* (of); *Maahu* (a chief who engaged the rainbow god in conflict). The hairs of Maahu. They are represented by the flax that grows on the cliff.

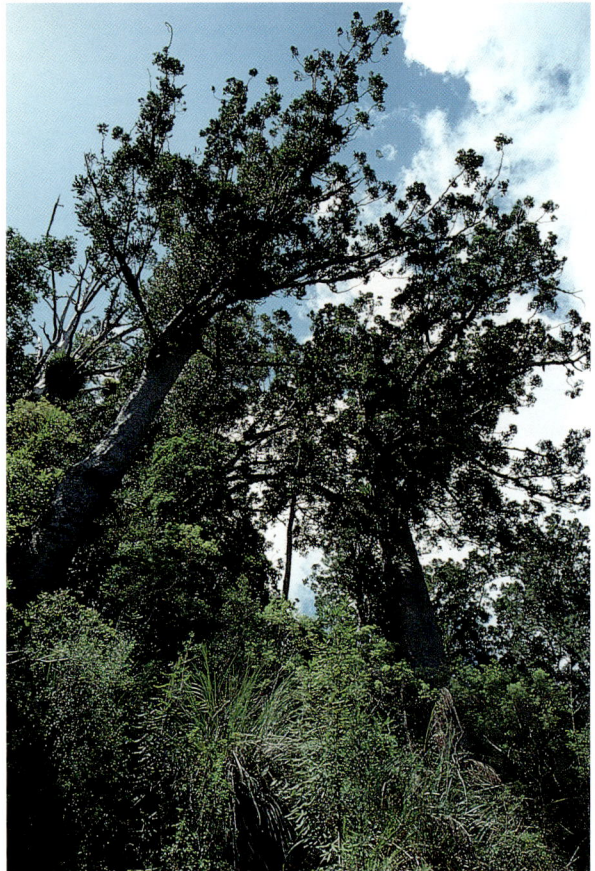

Ngāhere, the forest.

Ngāmatapōuri *ngā* (the); *matapōuri* (black teal).

Ngāmoana *ngā* (the); *moana* (pit-covers).

Ngāmoko *ngā* (the); *moko* (lizards).

Ngāmotu *ngā* (the); *motu* (islands).

Ngāone *ngā* (the); *one* (sands).

Ngāpaenga *ngā* (the); *paenga* (boundaries).

Ngā pākihi-whakatekateka-a-Waitaha *ngā* (the); *pākihi* (open plains); *whakatekateka* (to strut); *a* (of); *Waitaha* (South Island tribe). The plain where the Waitaha people gave vent to their joyful feeling in playful exuberance. This was the old name for the Canterbury Plains when they were first discovered.

Ngāpara The name should really be Ngātēpara. *Ngā* (the); *tēpara* (tables). It is a Pākehā invention, the equivalent of tablelands.

Ngāpōhatu *ngā* (the); *pōhatu* (rocks). The rocks.

Ngā poitu-o-te-Kupenga-a-Taramainuku The floats of the net of Taramainuku. These are the islands of the Hauraki Gulf. See Te Kupenga-a-Taramainuku.

Ngāpuhi *ngā* (the); *puhi* (plumes). The decorative plumes at the bow of a war canoe. Also the name of the North Auckland tribe.

Ngāpuke *ngā* (the); *puke* (hills).

Ngāpuna *ngā* (the); *puna* (springs).

Ngāroma *ngā* (the); *roma* (currents).

Ngāroto *ngā* (the); *roto* (lakes).

Ngāruawāhia *ngā* (the); *rua* (pits); *wāhia* (broken into). The plundered kūmara pits. The local tribe was entertaining a large party of visitors, and the store-pits of kūmara (sweet potatoes) had to be broken into to provide sufficient food.

Ngātaki *ngā* (the); *taki* (flocks of whiteheads: birds).

Ngatamiro *ngata* (dry); *miro* (tree). Dry miro tree.

Ngātapa *ngā* (the); *tapa* (edges).

Ngātīmoti Belonging to Timothy. A Māori carved his name on a tree. The words were *nā Tīmoti*, which means Belonging to Timothy, but they were changed to Ngātīmoti because it looked more like a Māori word.

Ngātira *ngā* (the); *tira* (parties of travellers).

Ngā tūāhu *ngā* (the); *tūāhu* (sacred places).

Ngā tutu-māhanga-a-Kau-kohea The twin tutu heads of Kau-kohea. When crossing the summit of a hill, a chief killed a hawk that was flying over with a sweep of his club. Not to be outdone, the other, Kau-kohea, made a slash at two tutu bushes growing there, and gave the name.

Ngāruawāhia, at the confluence of the Waipa and Waikato Rivers.

Ngāuranga *ngā* (the); *uranga* (people who came by canoe).

Ngāuruhoe The name of a slave girl (Auruhoe) who was thrown into the crater to appease the gods. There are also two literal translations. One is based on the story that Ngātoro-i-rangi threw his grandson Hoe into the crater, and the plumes of smoke represent his hair. *Ngā* (the); *uru* (hairs); *Hoe* (Ngātoro's grandson). The hairs of Hoe. The other gives the meaning as *ngā* (the); *uru* (the act of arranging hot stones in a *hangi*: oven); *hoe* (to toss out). When the mountain is erupting it tosses out hot stones.

Ngāurukehu *ngā* (the); *urukehu* (fair-haired people). The place of this name in Nelson was The red hairs, because a chief likened the prolific growth of the flax to his own red hair.

Ngāwaka *ngā* (the); *waka* (canoes).

Ngāwapurua *ngā* (the); *awa* (waters); *purua* (blocked up). The blocked-up waters. An alternative, Ngāwaipūrua, meaning The meeting of the waters, has been suggested.

Ngāwari Soft.

Ngāwaro *ngā* (the); *waro* (burning coals).

Ngāwhā

Ngāuruhoe, National Park.

Ngāwhā Boiling springs.

Ngāwhakapakoko *ngā* (the); *whakapakoko* (carved posts or palisades).

Ngā whatu *ngā* (the); *whatu* (eyes). When the Māori passed these rocks in Cook Strait, they veiled the eyes of those who were passing them for the first time, as otherwise the voyagers would meet with disaster. Another version is that Kupe placed the eyeballs of the octopus he killed on The Brothers, which thus became a tapu or sacred place.

Ngawi Native grass.

Ngongotahā *ngongo* (to drink); *tahā* (calabash). To drink from a calabash. Ihenga ascended this mountain and met a fairy woman who gave him a drink from her calabash. Then he was afraid and ran away, but gave the name to the river and mountain.

Ngunguru To sigh or to groan.

Ngutunui *ngutu* (lip); *nui* (big). Big lip.

Ngutuwera *ngutu* (lip); *wera* (burnt). Burnt lips.

Nihomanga *niho* (thorn); *manga* (stream). Thorny stream.

Nihoniho Young shoots or buds.

Nihotupu *niho* (tooth); *tupu* (broken). Decayed or broken teeth.

Nīkau Native palm.

Nīkau palms, Punakāiki.

Nokomai A corruption of Nukumai. Move this way towards the person speaking.

Nūhaka A place name which comes from Hawaiki. There is no Māori equivalent.

Nukuhou *nuku* (to move); *hou* (feather). Moving feather.

Nukunuku To move away.

Nukuroa Far-stretching land. An old name for the North Island.

O

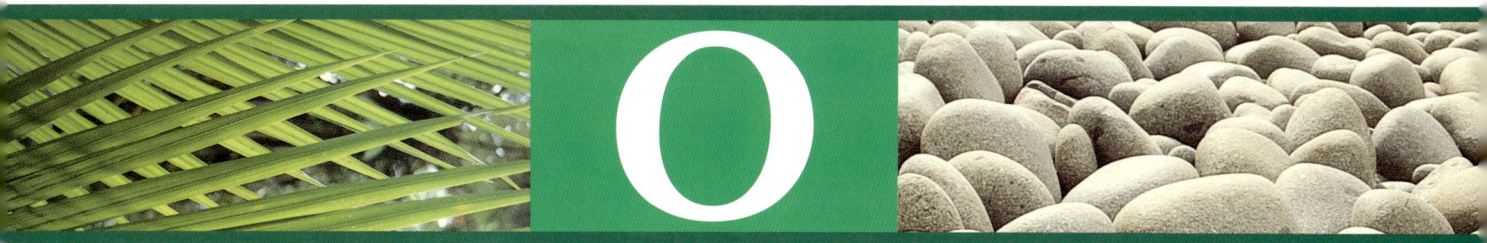

Ōakura The place of the flashing of the redness. Turi of the Aotea canoe had a red cloak, which when spread out at this place was a symbol of his mana (prestige).

Ōamaru The place of the god Maru.

Ōamaru stone buildings.

Ōamuru The place of the flesh left to dry. The flesh of conquered warriors was brought here to be preserved.

Ōaonui *ō* (the place of); *ao* (cloud); *nui* (big). The place of a large cloud.

Ōaro *ō* (the place of); *aro* (bog). A boggy place.

Ōeo *ō* (the place of); *eo* (louse). The place of lice.

Ōhaeawai The place of thermal water.

Ōhai *ō* (the place of); *hai* (stone used in a game).

Ohakēā *oha* (to repeat incantations); *kēā* (a lie, or false). Imperfect incantations.

Ōhakune *ō* (the place of); *hakune* (to be careful). A place to be careful in. Hakune is probably a personal name.

Ōhariu The correct name is Ōwhariu. It means The place where Kupe turned aside to dry the sails of his canoe.

Ōhau The place of Hau, a noted traveller or name-giver. His full name was Haunui-a-Nania. Elsewhere the name means Windy place. Ōhau Stream in Rotorua was the place of Ihenga's dog, Hau, who was drowned in a whirlpool.

Ōhaupō The place of Haupō. Or, *ō* (the place of); *hau* (wind); *pō* (night). The place of night winds.

Ōhawe *ō* (the place of); *hawe* (bend in a river or road).

Ohia To approve, or to think on the spur of the moment.

Ohikanui To perform rites with incantations. Two bands of warriors separated here, and one party was provided with food. The incantations were chanted to secure their return.

Ōhinehoe The place of Hinehoe. Literally, the place of an unpleasant girl.

Ōhinekōpiri *ō* (the place of); *hine* (girl); *kōpiri* (shrivelled). The place of a young girl. Her name was Punohu. She was assaulted, and her father died in her defence. Her body was hidden in a kūmara pit, but was revealed by the presence of hawks, and she was avenged.

Ōhinemutu *ō* (the place of); *hine* (girl); *mutu* (cut off). The place of the young woman who was killed. Hine-te-kakara (The fragrant maid) was the daughter of Ihenga. She was killed and thrown into a boiling mud pool. To punish the murderers, Ihenga set up a memorial stone and called it Ōhinemutu.

Ōhinemutu church on the shores of Lake Rotorua.

Ōhinepanea The place of Hinepanea.

Ōhinerau The place of Hinerau. She was a female goddess of whirlwinds.

Ōhinerēhia The place of Hinerēhia, who was a legendary mermaid.

Ōhinetahi The place of one daughter (daughter of Manuwhiri).

Ōhinewai The place of Hinewai. Literally, The place of the water girl.

Ōhingahape The place of the crooked foot. Named by Tiri after the crooked foot of Tua-nui-a-te-rā.

Ohingaiti The place of Hingaiti. Literally, *ohinga* (childhood); *iti* (small, or unimportant).

Ōhiro *ō* (the place of); *hiro* (dark, or stormy). A stormy place. The correct spelling is ōwhiro, and it may commemorate Whiro, the explorer.

Ōhiwa *ō* (the place of); *hiwa* (watchful, or alert). The place of watching.

Ōhoka *ō* (the place of); *hoka* (stake to which a decoy parrot is tied).

Ōhotu The place of Hotu. Literally, *ō* (the place of); *hotu* (the fifteenth night of the moon).

Ōhoukākā *ō* (the place of); *hou-kākā* (parrot feather). The place of the parrot's feather. Ihenga took a feather from his hair and stuck it in the ground, and it became a taniwha (water monster).

Ōhura The place of Hura. Literally, *ō* (the place of); *hura* (to uncover).

Ōihi *ō* (the place of); *ihi* (power, or authority).

Ōio *ō* (the place of); *io* (a spur).

Ōkā *ō* (the place of); *kā* (to burn). The place of burning or cooking. This was Shelly Beach, Auckland. Great catches of fish were made in the Waitematā and the people camped on the beach and kept the cooking fires going.

Okahau *oka* (knife); *hau* (famous). Famous knife.

Ōkahukura *ō* (the place of); *kahu* (garment); *kura* (red). The place of the red garment. Kahukura was the god of the rainbow.

Ōkaiawa *ō* (the place of); *kai* (food); *awa* (river). The place of food by the river, or in the valley.

Ōkaihau *ō* (the place of); *kaihau* (vagabond). Literally, one who eats wind.

Ōkarahia The place of calling in vain. Some fugitives were surprised and killed here.

Ōkaramio Correctly, Ōkuramio, the place of the plume of the miromiro (tomtit).

Ōkareka *ō* (food for a journey); *kareka* (sweet). Tasty food for travellers.

Ōkārito *ō* (the place of); *kārito* (bulrush). A place where bulrushes grow plentifully.

Ōkataina *ō* (the place of); *kataina* (laughter). The place of laughing. The full name is Te Moana-i-kataina-e-Te-Rangitakaroro, The ocean laughed at by Te Rangitakaroro. It has been suggested humorously that Rangitakaroro may well have laughed at the thought of the tiny Lake Ōkataina being described as an ocean.

Ōkarito beach, West Coast.

Ōkato The place of Kato. Literally, The place of the tidal wave, or the full-flowing tide.

Ōkau *ō* (the place of); *kau* (swimming or wading). The swimming place.

Ōkauia The place of Kauia. Literally, The place of articles threaded on a stick.

Ōkere *ō* (the place of); *kere* (to drift, or float).

Ōkete-upoko *ō* (the place of); *kete* (basket); *upoko* (head). The place where baskets full of human heads were kept. The famous warrior Te Rangi-whakaputa captured the locality of Lyttelton from the Ngāti-Māmoe and kept the heads of the slain in baskets.

Ōkete-upoko, now Lyttelton Harbour, Canterbury.

Ōkiato *ō* (the place of); *kiato* (a receptacle for holding sacred objects).

Ōkiore *ō* (the place of); *kiore* (rat).

Ōkiwi *ō* (the place of); *kiwi* (native flightless bird). The place of the kiwi.

Ōkoke *ō* (the place of); *koke* (moving forwards).

Ōkoki The place of the Koki canoe, which belonged to early inhabitants of New Zealand. *Koki* (small canoe).

Ōkonga *ō* (the place of); *konga* (running waters).

Ōkoroire *ō* (the place of); *koroire* (an extinct duck, which once was plentiful here).

Okowhiu *oko* (wooden bowl); *whiu* (to throw, or place). To place a wooden bowl. An Ārai-te-uru name.

Ōkūī *ō* (the place of); *kūī* (an underground insect). This is a very old name, because Kui was supposed to be one of the first people to live in New Zealand. He was an immediate descendant of Tuputupuwhenua, who was left in New Zealand by Māui.

Ōkuku *ō* (the place of); *kuku* (shining cuckoo). The Pākehā called the place Cuckoo Hills and this was changed to 'Māori' form, Ōkuku. Kuku is not the wood pigeon, therefore, but the shining cuckoo.

Ōkupe *ō* (the place of); *Kupe* (the famous explorer).

Ōkupu *ō* (the place of); *kupu* (message).

Ōkurī *ō* (the place of); *kurī* (dog).

Ōkuru *ō* (the place of); *kuru* (weary). The place of weariness.

Ōmāhanui *ō* (the place of); *māha* (pleasure); *nui* (great). The place of happiness.

Ōmahu The place of Mahu. Literally, The place of healing.

Ōmāhuri *ō* (the place of); *māhuri* (young trees).

Ōmahuta *ō* (the place of); *mahuta* (to rise). The place of rising, or landing from a canoe.

Ōmāio *ō* (the place of); *māio* (calm). A calm spot.

Ōmaka *ō* (the place of); *maka* (South Island form of *manga*: stream).

Ōmakau Belonging to husband and wife, i.e. the baby. There are three rocks here: the father, the mother, and the smallest, Ōmakau.

Ōmāmari The place of the Māmari canoe. This famous canoe, which came from Hawaiki, was wrecked at Maunganui Bluff, and is petrified as a group of rocks.

Ōmanaia *ō* (the place of); *manaia* (carved figure with beak).

Ōmānawa *ō* (the place of); *mānawa* (mangrove).

Ōmanu *ō* (the place of); *manu* (birds).

Ōmāpere *ō* (the place of); *māpere* (a species of *toetoe* plume grass).

Ōmarama The place of Marama. Literally, *ō* (the place of); *marama* (moon, or light).

Ōmatā *ō* (the place of); *matā* (quartz).

Ōmāui *ō* (the place of); *Māui* (the great explorer).

Ōnetahua, or Farewell Spit.

Ōmihi *ō* (the place of); *mihi* (lamentations). The place of this name in Canterbury was originally Omimi.

Ōmimi *ō* (the place of); *mimi* (a stream).

Ōmoana *ō* (the place of); *moana* (the ocean).

Ōmokoroa The place of Mokoroa. Literally, *ō* (the place of); *mokoroa* (a large white grub).

Ōnaeroa *ō* (the place of); *naeroa* (mosquito).

Ōnamalutu Obviously an incorrect spelling. It is probably Ōnamahutu, the place of a cave, and it has been suggested that as the entrance to the valley is narrow, it has something of the appearance of a cave.

Ōnawe The place set on fire. Te Rauparaha set fire to this village on the Ōnawe Peninsula in Akaroa Harbour.

Ōnehunga *ō* (the place of); *nehunga* (burial). There were burial places on the shore.

Onekakā *one* (sand); *kakā* (hot). A descriptive name.

Onekakara *one* (beach); *kakara* (cockle shell, or smelly). Either Cockle shell beach, or Smelly beach. As the beach at Waikouaiti was part of a whaling station, it would certainly have had an evil smell.

Onepoto *one* (beach); *poto* (short). Short, sandy beach.

Onepū *one* (sand); *pū* (loose). Loose sand.

Onepua Foam of the sea.

Onerahi *one* (beach); *rahi* (extensive). Long, sandy beach.

Oneroa *one* (beach); *roa* (long). Long beach.

Onetahua *one* (sand); *tahua* (heaped up). The name for Farewell Spit, and the sand dunes.

Onetahuti *one* (sand); *tahuti* (to run along). Running along the beach.

Onetangi *one* (sand); *tangi* (sounding). The sounding sands.

Onetapu *one* (sand); *tapu* (sacred). Sacred sand.

Onetea *one* (sand); *tea* (white). White sand.

Onewhero *one* (beach); *whero* (red). Red beach.

Ongaonga Nettle.

Ōngāroto *ō* (the place of); *ngā* (the); *roto* (lakes). The place of the lakes.

Ōngarue *ō* (the place of); *ngarue* (shaking, as in an earthquake).

Ōniao *ō* (the place of); *niao* (gunwale of a canoe).

Ōnoke *ō* (the place of); *noke* (earthworm).

Ōpaheke *ō* (the place of); *paheke* (slip). The place where the slip occurred.

Ōpaki *ō* (the place of); *paki* (fine weather).

Ōpapa *ō* (the place of); *papa* (flat land).

Ōpara *ō* (the place of); *para* (mud). Muddy place.

Ōpārae *ō* (the place of); *pārae* (open country).

Ōparapara *ō* (the place of); *parapara* (scum on the beach).

Ōpārara *ō* (the place of); *pārara* (to lie open towards). The shallow bay faces the Tasman Sea.

Ōpārau *ō* (the place of); *pā* (fortified village); *rau* (many). The place of many fortified villages.

Ōpatu *ō* (the place of); *patu* (to strike). The place of striking.

Ōpawa The correct form of the name is Ōpaawaho, The place of the outer or seaward *pā* (fortified village). This is the meaning of the name of Christchurch's Ōpawa. The Ōpawa River in Marlborough is said to be Ōpaoa, Smoky river, because of its appearance due to the brown swamp water which poured into it.

Ōpepe *ō* (the place of); *pepe* (moth).

Ōpihi *ō* (the place of); *pihi* (springing up, referring to plants). The place of good growth.

Ōpoho The place of Poho. Literally, *ō* (the place of); *poho* (chest, or stomach).

Ōponae *ō* (the place of); *ponae* (a small basket).

Ōpononi The place of Pononi.

Hokianga Harbour, Ōpononi.

Ōpōtiki The place of Pōtiki. He was Pōtiki-mai-Tawhiti, Pōtiki from Tahiti. Literally, The place of children.

Ōpōuri *ō* (the place of); *pōuri* (sadness).

Ōpoutama The place of Poutama. Literally, *ō* (the place of); *poutama* (pattern on the reed walls of a house).

Ōpoutere *ō* (the place of); *pou* (post); *tere* (to float). The place of the floating post.

Ōpua The place of Pua. Literally, *ō* (the place of); *pua* (flower).

Ōpuatia *ō* (the place of); *pua* (flowers); *tia* (to stick in). The place of adorning with flowers.

Ōpunake The place of Punake. Literally, *ō* (the place of); *punake* (bow of a canoe).

Ōpura *ō* (the place of); *pura* (dust in the eye). The place where Tamatea got dust in his eye.

Ōpūrere The place of flying mist.

Ōrākau *ō* (the place of); *rākau* (trees).

Ōrākei *ō* (the place of); *rākei* (adorning).

Ōrākei Wharf and Rangitoto Island, Auckland.

Ōrākei-kōrako *ō* (the place of); *rākei* (adorning); *kōrako* (white sinter). This beautiful hot pool with its glowing colours was used as a place where chiefs attended to their toilet.

Orana Correctly, Oranga: welfare.

Oranoa Escaping with difficulty.

Orapiu *ora* (alive, or escaped); *piu* (to throw).

Ōrarī The place of Rarī. Literally, *ō* (the place of); *rarī* (a fish).

Ōrātia *ō* (the place of); *rā* (sun); *tia* (persistency). The place of the long-lingering sun.

Orawaite When Reuben Waite, the first storekeeper on the West Coast, arrived with supplies for the gold-diggers, the Māori called joyfully, 'Ora, Waite!' This may be a contraction of 'Kia ora, Waite!' ('Welcome, Waite!') See also Orowaiti.

Orepuki

Orepuki Favourable weather; or, *aropi ki* (a cliff washed by high tides). A party of Māori was once drowned here when trying to pass at high tide.

Ōrere *ō* (the place of); *rere* (the waterfall, or low tide).

Ōreti *ō* (the place of); *reti* (a snare).

Ōrewa *ō* (the place of); *rewa* (the rewa shrub).

Orikākā *ori* (to wave to and fro); *kākā* (native parrot). To wave to attract the kākā. One method of snaring the kākā was to wave a piece of coloured fabric to attract the attention of the inquisitive bird, which was then easily caught. The Orikākā River was a place noted for birds.

Orikaroro *ori* (bad weather); *karoro* (seagull). Where seagulls congregate in bad weather.

Ōringi The place of Ringi (Rangi). The inhabitants of a besieged pā included a beautiful young woman who was admired by Takarangi of another tribe. When he heard that the defenders were short of water he walked boldly to the palisades with a calabash of water for the young woman. This ultimately brought peace, and joy to the lovers. At the spring there was once a sign that read, 'Kote Puna Oringi' (Being the spring of Ringi).

Other places of this name probably mean *ō* (the place of); *ringi* (to pour out). The place of pouring out. Ōrini has the same meaning.

Ōrini See Ōringi.

ōrongo *ō* (the place of); *rongo* (round bay).

Orongorongo Correctly, Te Wai-o-Rongorongo. *Te* (the); *wai* (water, or stream); *o* (of); *Rongorongo* (the name of a woman). The stream of Rongorongo.

Ōropi *ō* (the place of); *ropi* (to cover up). The place of concealment. It may also be a Māori form of Europe.

Ōroroa *ō* (the place of); *roroa* (a shellfish).

Ōrotore *ō* (the place of); *roto* (inside); *re* (short for *repo*: swamp). The swamp dwellers. This was an almost humorous term applied to the Māori who lived along the banks of the River Avon in Christchurch. Although they lived in a swampy region they were well provided with eels and ducks.

View from Summit Road, Christchurch.

Ōrotorepo See Ōrotore.

Orowaiti See Orawaite. The Māori, when referring to Reuben Waite, may have called him Oro Waite: Old Waite. Another explanation is that the name may originally have been Ora-iti: Escaping with difficulty.

Ōrua *ō* (the place of); *rua* (a pit).

Ōruaiti *ō* (the place of); *rua* (pit); *iti* (little). The place of the little pit.

Ōruaiwi *ō* (the place of); *rua* (two, or pit); *iwi* (bone). The place of two bones, or The place of the pit containing bones.

Ōruanui *ō* (the place of); *rua* (pit); *nui* (big). The place of the large pit.

Ōruawairua *ō* (the place of); *rua* (two); *wairua* (soul, or spirit). The place of the two spirits.

Ōruru *ō* (the place of); *ruru* (morepork).

Orurutūmārō The immovable owl, the legendary name of a guardian of cultivations.

Ōtago Correctly, Ōtakou. *Ō* (the place of); *tākou* (red earth, or red ochre). The Ōtago Peninsula abounded in yellow earth which yielded red ochre when burnt. The southern pronunciation of 'k' approaches 'g' in sound, and was pronounced Ōtago by the whalers. The name was extended from the kaik (kainga) near Taiaroa Head to the harbour, and finally to the province.

Ōtāhāiiti The place of the little calabash.

Ōtahu *ō* (the place of); *tahu* (signal fire). The local Māori used to light fires on the peak to warn their neighbours of the approach of raiding parties.

Otahuhu *ota* (uncooked); *huhu* (grub). Eating of the huhu grub in an uncooked state. This was done by Waikato Māori who, on dragging their canoes across the portage, discovered several rotten tree trunks full of huhu grubs.

Otahuti *ota* (uncooked); *huti* (to pull out of the ground).

Ōtāika *ō* (the place of); *tāika* (to lie in a heap); or **Otaika**: *ota* (to eat raw); *ika* (fish).

Ōtākaro *ō* (the place of); *tākaro* (games or sports). The place of the sport. The original name of the Avon River, and the site of Hagley Park.

Ōtaki *ō* (the place of); *taki* (to stick in). The place where the staff was stuck in the ground by Hau, who was pursuing his wife.

Ōtākiri *ō* (the place of); *tākiri* (loosening, or making free of tapu).

Ōtaku *ō* (the place of); *taku* (slow and deliberate, or firm and solid).

Ōtakuwao The place where a bird was seen flying past a belt of trees.

Ōtamahua *ō* (the place of); *tama* (short for *tamariki*: children); *hua* (eggs). The place where children ate seagulls' eggs. This was the Māori name for Quail Island, where the gulls' eggs were a delicacy much esteemed by children as well as adults.

Otamangō *ota* (uncooked); *mangō* (shark).

Ōtamarākau *ō* (the place of); *tama rākau* (warriors, or the young men who carry weapons).

Ōtamarau *ō* (the place of); *Tamarau* (a legendary spirit who comes in whirlwinds).

Otamātāpio *ota* (uncooked); *mātā* (a plant); *pio* (many).

Ōtanamomo Correctly, Ōtānemoamoa. *Ō* (the place of); *tāne* (man); *moamoa* (spherical stone).

Ōtāne The moon on the twenty-seventh day, or, The place of man.

Ōtānenui *ō* (the place of); *tāne* (man); *nui* (big). The place of the big man.

Ōtāneuru *ō* (the place of); *tāne* (man); *uru* (to gather berries). The place where the man gathered berries.

Ōtangaroa *ō* (the place of); *Tangaroa* (god of the sea).

Ōtangihaku *ō* (the place of); *tangi* (to cry or lament); *haku* (to murmur).

Ōtangiwai *ō* (the place of); *tangi* (to sound, or weep); *wai* (water). The place of sounding or weeping waters.

Ōtara *ō* (the place of); *tara* (mountain peak, or spear).

Ōtaraia The place of Taraia, a Waitaha chief.

Ōtari *ō* (the place of); *tari* (snare). The place of bird snares. Wilton and Mount Tinakori were places noted for birds.

Ōtatara *ō* (the place of); *tatara* (to untie or loosen). Or **Otatara**: *ota* (unripe); *tara* (point). Green point has been suggested as the meaning, but this is unlikely.

Ōtaua *ō* (the place of); *taua* (war party).

Ōtautahi *ō* (the place of); *Tautahi* (short for a personal name, Te Pōtiki-tautahi). A name for the Avon River.

Ōtautau The place of Tautau. Literally, *ō* (the place of); *tautau* (greenstone ear-pendant with curved lower end).

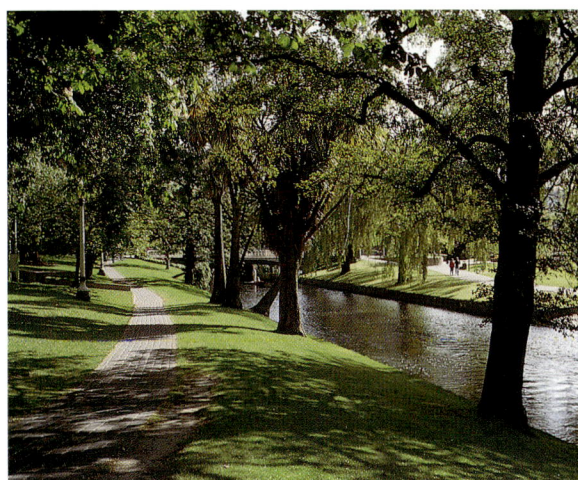

Ōtautahi, The Avon River, Christchurch.

Otautu *ota* (raw); *utu* (revenge). Raw revenge. After a battle fought to avenge a wrong, the victors ate raw the bodies of the vanquished.

Ōtawa *ō* (the place of); *tawa* (native tree). The place of tawa trees.

Ōtekaieke *ō* (of); *te* (the); *kaieke* (going around).

Ōtekura *ō* (the place of); *te* (the); *kura* (red feather). The place of the red feather.

Ōtematatā The place of good quartz or flint.

Ōtepopo The place of Te Popo. Literally, The place of the decay.

Ōtepoti *ō* (the place of); *te* (the); *poti* (corner, angle). The place situated at a corner. The name of a village near the present Exchange, in Dunedin.

The Dunedin Railway Station.

Ōtetī *ō* (the place of); *te* (the); *tī* (cabbage tree). The place of the cabbage tree.

Ōteuku *ō* (the place of); *te* (the); *uku* (white clay).

Ōtewā *ō* (the place of); *te* (the); *wā* (open country).

Ōtiake Correctly, Ōtiaki. *Ō* (the place of); *tiaki* (to watch for). The place of watching.

Ōtiki The place of the tiki (image) of Marokura.

Ōtipua *ō* (the place of); *tipua* (goblin).

Ōtira *ō* (the place of); *tira* (a company of travellers). There was an old camping place on the Ōtira River where food was prepared for the journey over the ranges by the Hurunui Pass.

Ōtiria *ō* (the place of); *tiria* (to be planted).

Ōtītaha *ō* (the place of); *tītaha* (the axe).

Ōtōkia The place of Tōkia. Literally, *ō* (the place of); *tōkia* (to be wet).

Ōtoko *ō* (the place of); *toko* (a stick).

Ōtonga *ō* (the place of); *tonga* (the south).

Ōtoroa The place of Toroa (a chief).

Ōtorohanga *ō* (food for a journey); *torohanga* (to cause to extend over a distance). Food eked out. A chief who was going to Taupō carried only a small quantity of food, which he made last out the journey by means of magic spells.

Totem poles, Ōtorohanga.

Ōtōtara *ō* (the place of); *tōtara* (native tree).

Ōtuhi *ō* (the place of); *tuhi* (smell of decaying fish).

Otūkoroiti Correctly, Okoroiti, the moon on the fifth day of the month. A fight that took place here began at sunrise on the fifth day and ended only when the moon rose.

Ōtūmahana The place of warm, still waters.

Otūmoetai The tide standing still as if asleep.

Otupaka *otu* (dried or scorched); *paka* (girdle).

Ōtūrehua *ō* (the place of); *tū* (to stand); *rehua* (a star). The place where the summer star stands high in the heavens, i.e. a place where it is very warm.

Ōtūtahanga *ō* (the place of); *tū* (to stand); *tahanga* (naked). The place of standing naked.

Ōue The place of Ue or Ui, who came to the South Island with Māui. Literally, a species of flax, or the moon on the fourth night.

Ōuruhia *ō* (the place of); *uruhia* (to be attacked).

Ōwahanga *ō* (the place of); *wahanga* (the entrance). The mouth of the river.

Ōwairaka The place of Wairaka, or The water of Raka.

Ōwairoa *ō* (the place of); *wai* (water); *roa* (long). The place of the long river, the old name for Howick.

Ōwaka *ō* (the place of); *waka* (canoe, or trough).

Ōwānanga The place of the historical recitals.

Ōwē *ō* (the place of); *Wē* or *Wī* (proper name), who came to the South Island with Māui.

Ōweka *ō* (the place of); *weka* (wood-hen). The place where the weka is plentiful.

Ōwhakatihi *Ō* (the place of); *whakatihi* (to pile up in a heap). The sons of Tūwharetoa ranged over the Kaingaroa Plain in search of someone to attack, but when they met a party of Māori they were defeated, and their bodies were piled up in a heap at the foot of a tree.

Ōwhango *ō* (the place of); *whango* (hoarse or nasal sound).

Ōwhāroa *ō* (food for a journey); *whāroa* (lasting a long time). It has much the same meaning as Ōtorohanga.

Ōwhata *ō* (the place of); *whata* (a food-store).

Ōwhiro *ō* (the place of); *whiro* (a moonless night, or the god of darkness).

Ōwhitiangaterā *ō* (the place of); *whitianga* (shining); *te* (the); *rā* (sun). The place of the shining sun.

P

Pā Fortified village. The name usually occurs in places named by Pākehā, such as Pā Flat.

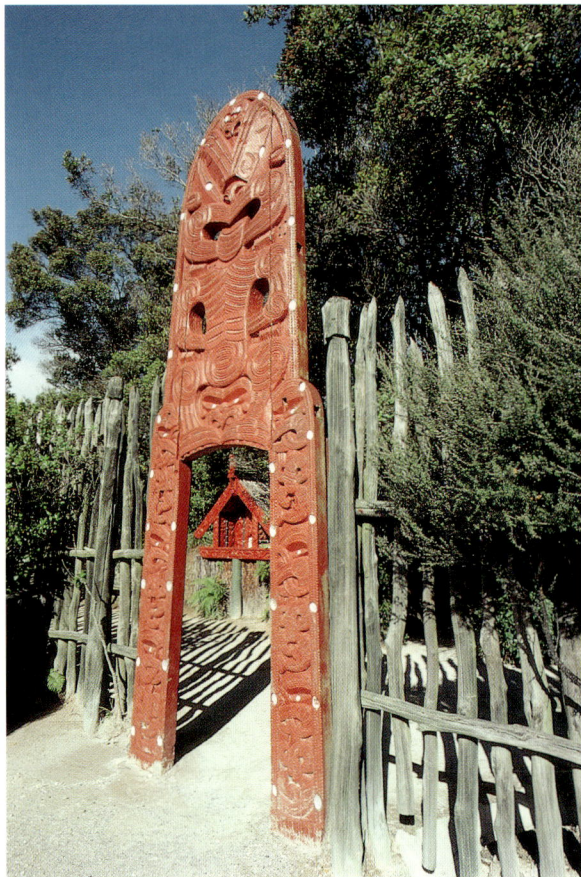

Carved gateway, Rotorua.

Paehinahina *pae* (headland); *hinahina* (whitey-wood). Headland clothed with hinahina, māhoe, or whitey-wood trees.

Paekākāriki *pae* (perch); *kākāriki* (parakeet). The perch of parakeets. There is a legend that Hau, who was pursuing his wife, came to a barrier of rock at the south end of the beach, which gave the name to the place. He made a hole in the cliff with his taiaha, and walked through to the other side, where he found his wife.

Paekohu The place of fogs.

Paenga Boundary, or the margin of the kūmara plantations.

Paengaroa *paenga* (boundary); *roa* (long). Long boundary or margin.

Paerātā *pae* (ridge); *rātā* (native tree). The ridge of the rātā tree. A large rātā stood here for many years, most of the surrounding trees being pūriri.

Paerau *pae* (step, or ridge); *rau* (a hundred, or many). A hundred ridges.

Paeroa *pae* (ridge, or range); *roa* (long). Long mountain range.

Paetawa *pae* (bird-snare); *tawa* (native tree). The tawa tree containing a bird-snare.

Paewhenua *pae* (dock, or long-rooted weed); *whenua* (country). Noxious weed country.

Pāharakeke *pā* (fortified village); *harakeke* (flax). Pā near which flax grows.

Pāhau Beard, or the withered, drooping lower leaves of the cabbage tree.

Pāhautāne Correctly, Pāhau-taniwha. *Pāhau* (whalebone); *taniwha* (large fish). A war party was retiring up the coast after a raid, and found to their dismay that their concealed food-stores had been plundered. They camped for the night and the next morning found a school of blackfish stranded on the beach. In their hunger, they ate the flesh raw. Taniwha is used for fish such as large sharks, and whales, as well as for fabulous water monsters.

Pāhautea *pāhau* (beard); *tea* (white). White beard.

Pahī Company of travellers.

Pāhia Slapped, or a preparation of mashed food.

Pahiatua *pahi* (resting place); *atua* (a god). The resting place of a god. A chief escaped from a fight, and was led by his atua on the flight until they came here and rested on the hill.

Pahitua *pahī* (company of travellers); *tua* (cut down). Party of travellers cut down.

Pāhoro *pā* (fortified village); *horo* (to evacuate). The pā that was hurriedly evacuated.

Paiatepukahu *pai* (good); *a* (of); *te* (the); *pukahu* (abundant). The place of good, abundant food.

Paihia Good here. It is believed to be a word of mixed origin. The Reverend Henry Williams came to New Zealand knowing only a few words of Māori, including pai, which means good. When they came to this place he turned to his companion, a Māori chief, and said, 'Pai here.' It is possible that the name should be Pāhia.

Paire A bundle.

Pākarae *pā* (fortified village); *karae* (sea bird). Sea bird village.

Pākaraka *pā* (fortified village); *karaka* (native tree). Village of the karaka tree.

Pākawau *pā* (flock, or colony); *kawau* (shag). Colony of shags.

Pākeha *pā* (garden plot); *keha* (indigenous white turnip). Plot where the turnip grows. One explanation of the name Pākehā is that it is one

whose skin is white like that of a turnip. There are other explanations which are not so polite.

Paihia, Bay of Islands.

Pākihi Flat land, usually dried up and poor.

Pākihikura *pākihi* (flat land); *kura* (red). Reddish-coloured flat land.

Pākihiroa *pākihi* (flat country); *roa* (long or broad). Large extent of pākihi.

Pakipaki An abbreviation of Pakipaki-o-Hinetemoa. This high-born young woman came to a stream accompanied by her slave girl. After she had bathed, her maid slapped (pakipaki) and massaged her body.

Pākira Bald head. Pākira-a-Hikawera was a place where a chief of this name was wearing a closely fitting hat of birds' feathers. Feeling hot, he took it off, and another chief exclaimed, 'What a beautiful bald head you have!'

Pakiri To grin.

Pakōtai *pakō* (to make a sudden sound); *tai* (the sea). Sudden sound from the sea.

Pākōwhai *pā* (fortified village); *kōwhai* (native tree). The pā by the kōwhai trees. Or **Pakowhai**: *pako* (to glean); *whai* (to search for). To look for remnants of the crop after it has been harvested.

Paku A small quantity.

Pakuranga *paku* (small quantity); *ranga* (company of persons, or shoal of fish). A small company, or a small shoal of fish.

Pamapuria The Māori pronunciation of Pamphylia,

a locality named by the Reverend Joseph Matthews of Kaitaia.

Pāngaio *pā* (fortified village); *ngaio* (native tree). Pā near the ngaio trees.

Pangatōtara *panga* (thrown); *tōtara* (native tree). Probably named because a tōtara log was left here after a flood.

Panguru To make a rumbling sound.

Pānia The Pānia Reef at Napier is named after a woman of the sea people who married a Māori chief.

Papa-aroha *papa* (foundation); *aroha* (love, or affection). The foundation of love. A meeting place for many scattered sub-tribes.

Pāpāhaoa A variety of kūmara.

Papahīnau *papa* (undulating or nearly flat land); *hīnau* (a native shrub). Flat where the hīnau grows. Also known as Papahina, and Papahinu.

Papaioea Popularly believed to mean, How beautiful it is! Another explanation is, *papai* (exceedingly good); *oea* (the beauty that comes on the water when dead bodies are soaked in it). The Rangitāne people were said to soak the bodies of the slain in water before storing or eating them. This place is the site of Palmerston North.

Papaiti *papa* (flat); *iti* (little). Little flat.

Papakaio *papa* (flat); *kaio* (South Island form of ngaio). Ngaio flat.

Papaki A cliff against which the waves beat.

Papakura *papa* (flat); *kura* (red). Level land of red soil.

Papamoa *papa* (flat); *moa* (raised beds). Level land with raised plots for cultivation.

Papanui Big flat plain, or a stage in a tree used as a seat by a bird-snarer.

Paparātā *papa* (flat); *rātā* (native tree). Rātā flat.

Paparekareka *papa* (flat rock); *rekareka* (pleasant). The name would mean Pleasant flat, but Paparekareka is a bluff in North Otago.

Paparimu *papa* (flat); *rimu* (native tree). Rimu flat.

Paparoa Long flat rock, or large expanse of level land. Where the name refers to a headland it means Long, flat, rocky point.

Papatawa *papa* (flat); *tawa* (native tree). Tawa flat.

Papatea Possibly named after the light-coloured papa-rock banks of the stream, or a term for a chief who was not tattooed.

Papatoetoe *papa* (flat); *toetoe* (pampas grass). Toetoe flat.

Papatōtara *papa* (flat); *tōtara* (native tree). Tōtara flat.

Papatōwai *papa* (flat); *tōwai* (native tree). Tōwai (or kāmahi) flat.

Papawai *papa* (flat land); *wai* (water). Inundated land.

Papaweka *papa* (flat); *weka* (wood-hen). Weka run, or fowl run. It sometimes appears as Tāpapaweka.

Formerly one of New Zealand's most common birds, the weka is now rare in the North Island and endangered in the South.

Pāponga *pā* (fortified village); *ponga* (fern). Pā by the fern trees.

Para A type of fern, or possibly swamp.

Parahaki A corruption of Parahaka, which is a contraction of Parawhau and haka. The Parawhau tribe had a large pā on the summit. They were invaded and defeated, and the conquerors danced a haka of triumph. Or, the invaders danced a haka prior to inviting the Parawhau to surrender.

Pāraharaha The name comes from a pool of black mud in which flax fibre was dyed.

Parahau Windy place.

Parakai *para* (fern-root); *kai* (food, or to eat).

Parakakau *para* (fern); *kakau* (stalk). Fern-stalk.

Parakao Dried kūmara.

Paranui *para* (fern); *nui* (big, or plenty). Plenty of fern.

Parapara Name of a Māori. Literally, Soft mud used in dyeing flax fibre.

Paraparaumu *parapara* (scraps, or waste fragments); *umu* (earth oven). A hungry taua (war party) captured a village but found only fragments of food in the oven. An earlier name may have been Paraparamāu, meaning First-fruits for you.

Pararoa Possibly should be Parāoa, as it is said that it means whale, because one was washed ashore here long ago.

Paratetaitonga Dregs from the southern seas.

Pārau Slave.

Pārawa *pā* (fortified village); *rawa* (property, or ground). Land on which the village was built.

Parawai A cloak, or sandal. The name comes from Tahiti and was given by Tama-te-kapua to his kūmara plantation in memory of those at Tahiti.

Parekākāriki *pare* (plume); *kākāriki* (parakeet). Plume of the kākāriki.

Parekura Red ornamental band for the forehead.

Paremata A return feast for one previously given.

Pāremoremo Hesitating, or slippery.

Parenga Properly Perongo, slippery, or stream with slippery banks.

Pārengarenga The renga lily, or the place where the lily grows.

Pareora Life-giving, or bountiful. The name may originally have been Pureora, a sacred rite performed for the recovery of the sick.

Pārera Native duck.

Paretai Bank of a river.

Pariawhakatahakura *pari* (cliff); *a* (of); *whakataha* (to cause to change direction); *kura* (red). The red lichen-covered cliff which causes the river to change direction.

Parihaka Low cliff.

Parikārakaraka Echoing cliff.

Parikawa Abbreviated form of Parikawakawa. *Pari* (cliff); *kawakawa* (native tree). Cliff where the kawakawa grows.

Parikawau *pari* (cliff); *kawau* (shag). Shag cliff.

Pāringa *pā* (blow); *ringa* (hand). To strike a blow with the hand.

Parininihi *pari* (cliff); *ninihi* (lofty). Lofty cliff. The White Cliffs were 800 feet (240 metres) in height.

Parinuioterā *pari* (cliff); *nui* (big); *o* (of); *te* (the); *rā* (sun). The big cliff shining in the sun.

Paripari Precipitous country.

Pariroa *pari* (cliff); *roa* (long, or tall). High cliff.

Pariruru *pari* (cliff); *ruru* (sheltered). Cliff which provides a shelter from the wind.

Paritea *pari* (cliff); *tea* (white). White or light-coloured cliff.

Paritutū *pari* (cliff); *tutū* (erect). Upright cliff.

Pariwhero *pari* (cliff); *whero* (red). Red cliff.

Pāroa *pā* (fortified village); *roa* (long). Spread out or straggling settlement.

Pārore Gentle, or friendly. Named after Pārore te Āwhā, who died in 1887 when he was nearly 100; he was always friendly to Pākehā.

Pārua *pā* (fortified village); *rua* (pit, or two). Two pā, or the pit in the pā.

Paruāuku Soil of white clay.

Paruparu Black mud used in dyeing flax fibre.

Pātara Māori pronunciation of Butler (or bottle).

Pātea In full, Pātea-nui-a-Turi. The place where Turi's people threw down their great burdens.

This monument to the war canoe Aotea commemorates the settlement of Pātea and the surrounding Taranaki area.

Pātearoa Abbreviated form of Pāwātea roa. Long fortification with a clear view.

Pāterangi *pā* (fortified village); *te* (the); *rangi* (sky). The fort in the sky.

Pātetonga *pā* (fortified village); *te* (the); *tonga* (south wind). Village swept by the south wind.

Pātoka The pā in the rocks. The hill above the pā has great limestone formations.

Patumāhoe *patu* (weapon, or to strike); *māhoe* (timber of a native tree). In a battle at this place a chief was killed with a māhoe stake.

Pātūnga *pā* (fortified village); *tūnga* (being wounded). The place where someone was wounded.

Paturuahine *patu* (to strike); *ruahine* (old woman). The place where the old woman was struck.

Pātūtahi *pā* (fortified village); *tūtahi* (lonely). Lonely or isolated village.

Pāua Shellfish.

Pāua was a common food source for the Maori. Today the beautiful shell is polished and used for jewellery.

Pāuatahanui Big shellfish.

Pehu Variety of kūmara, to pound, or to bend.

Peka Named after Peka Mākarini (Baker McLean).

Pekapekarau *pekapeka* (native bat); *rau* (many). The place where native bats were plentiful.

Pekatahi *peka* (branch); *tahi* (single). The single branch.

Pekerangi The outer palisades of a pā.

Peowhairangi The Māori pronunciation of Bay of Islands.

Pepeke Native butterfly.

Peraki Probably Pireka (which was the spelling adopted by the French), fern, the root of which had a pleasant smell when pounded.

Peria Māori form of the biblical Berea.

Pētane Māori pronunciation of Bethany. The name is now changed to Bay View to avoid confusion with Petone.

Peterehema Māori form of Bethlehem.

Petone A corruption of Pito-one. *Pito* (end); *one* (sandy beach). End of the beach.

Piaka Root of a tree, or weapon made from a root.

Piako Shrunk, or hollow. The name was brought from Hawaiki by the Tainui people.

Piha Ripple at the bow of a canoe.

Pihama After Hone Pihama. Literally, *piha* (ripple); *mā* (white).

Pihanga Window. The mountain had an opening in its side like the smoke vent in a house.

Pīhautea See Pahautea.

Pīkaroro *pī* (nestling); *karoro* (seagull). Nestling of seagulls.

Pikopiko Winding.

Pikowai *piko* (curving); *wai* (water). Curving stream.

Pininoa A refuge, or hiding place.

Piopio Native thrush.

Piopiotahi *piopio* (native thrush); *tahi* (single). A single thrush. This was the Māori name for Milford Sound. A legend says that after Māui was defeated by the goddess of death, the thrush fled here sorrowing for its dead companion. Another legend says it is the name of a very early canoe.

Pipi Shellfish.

Pipikarita Shellfish for evil spirits.

Pipiriki *pipi* (shellfish); *riki* (little). Little pipi. An old chief who was dying asked for little pipi, and a canoe was sent to get them, but by the time they arrived back he was dead.

Pipiroa *pipi* (shellfish); *roa* (long, or many). Plenty of pipi.

Pipitea *pipi* (shellfish); *tea* (white). White shellfish.

Pīpīwai Damp, or swampy.

Pīpīwharauroa The shining cuckoo.

Piriaka *piri* (to cling); *aka* (vine). The clinging forest vines.

Pirinoa A parasitic plant.

Piripai The Māori form of Philippi.

Piripaua *piri* (clinging); *pāua* (shellfish). The clinging shellfish. They are plentiful in the two places in Marlborough with this name.

Piripiri A burr, commonly known as biddybid.

Pirongia The full name is Pirongia-te-aroaro-o-Kahu, meaning The health-restoring purification of Kahurere, whose husband restored her to health.

Pōhāngina The warming of the ovens at night.

Pōhaturoa *pōhatu* (stone); *roa* (long). Long stones are found in the river bed in Westland. Elsewhere it means The tall rock.

Pōhutu geyser, Whakarewarewa.

Pohokura The name of a chief. Literally, *poho* (breast); *kura* (red).

Pohonui The big haul.

Pohowahine *poho* (breast); *wahine* (woman). A woman's breast.

Pohowaikawa *poho* (breast); *waikawa* (bitter water).

Pōhuehue Climbing plant, such as convolvulus.

Pōhuenui *pōhue* (convolvulus); *nui* (big, or many). Plenty of convolvulus.

Pōhutu Splashing. The famous geyser at Whakarewarewa.

Pohutukawa Native tree with scarlet blossoms. The name is usually given by Pākehā, as in Pohutukawa Flat.

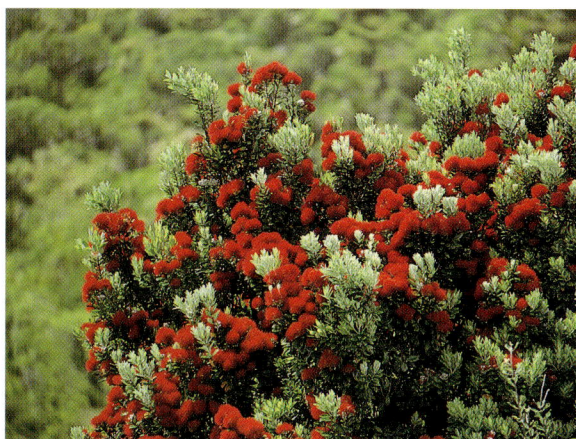

The pohutukawa is New Zealand's Christmas tree.

Poka The name of a pet lizard lost at this place by Tamatea.

Pōkaikōkō Flock of tūī.

Pōkaiwhenua A wanderer across the land. It is a tributary of the Waikato River.

Pōkākā A tree related to the hīnau.

Pokapū Middle, or a house with the door in the middle of its side wall.

Pōkeno Turbid; or *pō* (night); *keno* (underworld). Night in the underworld.

Pokere Pulp of the tawa berry, or pitfall, or in the dark.

Pokohiwi Name of a chief. Literally, shoulder.

Pokopokoiere Native frog.

Pokororo Abbreviation for upokororo, native fish (grayling).

Pōmahaka Correctly, Pou-mahaka, posts to which snares are attached.

Pōmare Named after Sir Māui Pōmare.

Pōneke Māori form of Port Nick, a contraction of Port Nicholson.

Ponga Tree-fern.

Pongakawa To devour. Also *ponga* (tree-fern); *kawa* (bitter).

Pongaroa Name of a game; or, *ponga* (tree-fern); *roa* (long, or many). Plenty of tree-ferns.

Pōnui *pō* (night); *nui* (big). Big night.

Popoia A gathering together.

Pōpōtūnoa Correctly, Poupoutūnoa, a post set up to mark the boundaries between Ngāti-Māmoe and Ngāi-Tahu.

Pōrangahau *pō* (night); *rangahau* (pursuit). The inhabitants of Heretaunga once had to make a hasty retreat from their enemies to this place.

Porangarua The correct form of the name is Pungarehu, ashes left by the fire. Some fugitives were discovered here when the wind stirred up the ashes of their fire.

Pōrangirangi To annoy at night.

Poranui *pora* (flat-roofed); *nui* (big).

Porararī Correctly, Pororarī. *Poro* (broken off); *rarī* (uproar). The end of the uproar. The waters of the river would rise swiftly and turbulently, and recede as quickly.

Pōrewa Elevated platform or watch-tower.

Porirua The proper form is probably Parirua. *Pari* (flowing tide); *rua* (two). There are two arms in the harbour. It may also be named after the taniwha which was supposed to inhabit it.

Poro-o-Tarao The posterior of Tarao. The chief was climbing the range ahead of his companions with his rāpaki (waist-mat) kilted up, and the sight amused his companions who were below him.

Poroporo A plant with a blue flower.

Porotī A forest bird; or *poro* (to cut short); *tī* (cabbage tree).

Pōtaka After Utiku Pōtaka. Literally, a spinning top.

Pōteriteri Dripping wet. Or Poutiritiri, a post on which offerings are hung, which is the more likely meaning.

Pōterīwhi Port of relief.

Pōtete A small bark basket.

Pouākai A fabulous gigantic bird.

Poukawa *pou* (post); *kawa* (lean). Lean pole. Of the two chiefs who lived by the lake, one was more powerful than the other. The lesser chief asked that their fishing boundaries be divided, but the great chief was insulted. Then the lesser chief put a pole dividing the boundary, giving himself the best part of the lake, and leaving the tuna kawa (lean eels) for the other. The lake was then called Lean pole. Much strife followed.

Poukino *pou* (post); *kino* (bad).

Pounamu Greenstone.

Pounawea *pou* (post); *nawea* (to set on fire). Post which was set on fire.

Poutini A form of greenstone. It is the 'fish' which Kupe brought with him from Hawaiki, and was once the name for the whole of the West Coast.

Pōuto To cut off.

Poutū *pou* (staff); *tū* (to stand). Staff standing up. When Tamatea reached this place on the east side of Lake Taupō, he rested on his staff while he surveyed the district.

Pōwaru *pō* (night); *waru* (eight). Eight nights. Tamatea and his men dragged their canoe overland from the headwaters of the Whanganui to Lake Taupō. At this place they were unable to obtain provisions and had to go for eight days and nights without food.

Pūaha Mouth of a river.

Puatai Foam of the sea.

Puha A war song, or a wild vegetable.

Puhinui *puhi* (plumes); *nui* (big). Great plume at the bow of a canoe. It is the name of a canoe, and the settlement near Papatoetoe. It is also an early name for Warkworth, where it means Great promise, i.e. engagement or betrothal.

Pūhoi Slow water, so-called because the tide is very slow in creeping up the river to make it navigable for canoes.

Pukaha Spongy or swampy.

Pūkaki Head of the creek, or where the stream meets the tidal waters. Lake Pūkaki may have this meaning, but there is a legend that Rākaihautū (who scooped out the southern lakes) saw its bulging outlet and called it *pū* (heaped or bunched up), and *kakī* (neck).

Lake Pūkaki.

Pukapuka Shrub with white leaves.

Pūkaramū A clump of karamū trees.

Pukatea A native tree.

Pukearuhe *puke* (hill); *aruhe* (fern-root). Hill where fern-root may be found.

Pukeatua *puke* (hill); *atua* (god). The hill of the god.

Pukehāpopo *puke* (hill); *hāpopo* (corpse of an enemy). The hill of the enemy corpse. A name that comes from the Society Islands.

Pukehiki *puke* (hill); *hiki* (charm to raise anything from the water). Hill of the incantation.

Pukehina *puke* (hill); *hina* short for *hinahina*: small tree, māhoe, or whitey-wood. Hill of the māhoe tree.

Pukehīnau *puke* (hill); *hīnau* (native tree). Hill of the hīnau trees.

Pukehiwitahi *puke* (hill); *hiwi* (peak); *tahi* (single). Hill with a single peak. It was named after the captain of the Ārai-te-uru canoe, and is now known as Pukeviti.

Pukehou *puke* (hill); *hou* (short for *houhou*: small flowering tree). Hill of the houhou trees. Pukehou in Horowhenua is the hill of dedication, where a boy was dedicated to the recovery of his tribal lands.

Pukehuhu *puke* (hill); *huhu* (grub). Hill where the huhu grubs were to be found.

Pukehuia *puke* (hill); *huia* (extinct native bird). Hill of the huia.

Pukekākāriki *puke* (hill); *kākāriki* (parakeet). Hill of the parakeets.

Pukekāhu *puke* (hill); *kāhu* (hawk). Hill of the hawks.

Pukekaihau *puke* (hill); *kaihau* (a ceremony performed over successful warriors when they returned). Hill where victory is celebrated.

Pukekāpia *puke* (hill); *kāpia* (kauri gum). Kauri gum hill.

Pukekaroro *puke* (hill); *karoro* (seagull). Hill where the seagulls gather. It was a fortified hill which frequently changed hands, and after each battle the seagulls gathered in their thousands.

Pūkeko A swamp bird.

Pukekohe *puke* (hill); *kohe* short for *kohekohe*: a native tree. Hill where the kohekohe tree grows.

Pukekoikoi *puke* (hill); *koikoi* (pointed). Pointed hills, or a sharp-ridged hill.

Pukekōmā *puke* (hill); *kōmā* (light-coloured). A hill that is light in colour.

Pukekura *puke* (hill); *kura* (red). Red hill.

Pukekurī *puke* (hill); *kurī* (dog). Hill of dogs.

Pukemāeroero *puke* (hill); *māeroero* (wild men). Hill of the wild men.

Pukemaire *puke* (hill); *maire* (native tree). Maire hill.

Pukemakariri *puke* (hill); *makariri* (cold). Cold hill.

Pukemāori *puke* (hill); *Māori* (native). Māori hill.

Pukemata *puke* (hill); *mata* (headland). The hill on the headland.

Pukemātāwai *puke* (hill); *mātāwai* (source of waters). The hill which is the source of several streams or rivers. This name was given in recent years because the hill in the Tararua Range is the source of a number of rivers.

Pukemiro *puke* (hill); *miro* (native tree). Miro hill.

Pukemoa *puke* (hill); *moa* (large extinct, flightless bird). Moa hill. So named because it was a haunt of the moa long ago, as is shown by the presence of bones.

Pukenamu *puke* (hill); *namu* (sandfly). Sandfly hill.

Pukengerengere *puke* (hill); *ngerengere* (leprosy or skin disease). Hill where a sufferer from leprosy was isolated.

Pukenui *puke* (hill); *nui* (big). Big hill.

Pukeokaoka *puke* (hill); *okaoka* (South Island form of *ongaonga*: nettle). Hill where the nettles grow.

Pukeone *puke* (hill); *one* (sand). Sandy-topped hill.

Pukeowara *puke* (hill); *o* (of); *Wara* (Ward). Named after Sir Joseph Ward.

Pukepoto Dark blue earth used as a pigment. It is found in the nearby swamp.

Pukerangi *puke* (hill); *rangi* (sky). Hill that reaches up into the sky.

Pukerau *puke* (hill); *rau* (many). Many hills.

Pukerauaruhe *puke* (hill or mound); *rau* (many); *aruhe* (fern-root). A great heap of fern-root.

Pukerimu *puke* (hill); *rimu* (native tree). Rimu hill.

Pukeroa *puke* (hill); *roa* (long). Long hill.

Pukerua *puke* (hill); *rua* (two). Two hills.

Puketā *puke* (hill); *tā* (sloping). Sloping hill. It is possible that the name is a corruption of peketa (dart).

Puketai Literally, *puke* (hill); *tai* (sea). The hill of Tai. It may mean Hill across the water. Puketai, which is the site of Andersons Bay, Dunedin, should be Puketahi, The first hill, i.e. the first of a series of hills down the peninsula.

Puketapu *puke* (hill); *tapu* (sacred). Sacred or forbidden hill.

Puketarata *puke* (hill); *tarata* (native tree). Lemonwood tree hill.

Puketawai *puke* (hill); *tawai* (native tree). Tawai hill.

Puketeraki *puke* (hill); *te* (the); *raki* (South Island form of *rangi*: sky). Hill reaching up to the sky. The proper form of the name is Puketiraki, tiraki meaning lifting sharply skywards.

Puketihi *puke* (hill); *tihi* (top). Top of the hill. From this peak the three mountains of Tongariro National Park can be seen on a clear day.

Puketiro *puke* (hill); *tiro* (view). Hill with an extensive view from the summit.

Puketitiro *puke* (hill); *titiro* (view). Hill with a commanding view.

Puketoi *puke* (hill); *toi* (summit). Summit of the hill.

Puketona *puke* (hill); *tona* (mound).

Puketōtara *puke* (hill); *tōtara* (native tree). Totara hill.

Puketūī *puke* (hill); *tūī* (native bird). Tūī hill.

Puketutu *puke* (hill); *tutu* (native tree). Tutu hill. There are several places of this name, and in some, as in Weeks Island, tutu is the tree; in others it is a plant.

Pukeuri Named after a woman on the Ārai-te-uru canoe. Literally, *puke* (hill); *uri* (dark). Dark hill.

Pukewāhia Firewood hill. Literally, *puke* (hill); *wāhia* (split, or divided). Split hill.

Pukewhero *puke* (hill); *whero* (red). Red hill. Named by a party in 1932 because the last few hundred feet are a jumble of bright-red rocks.

Pūkorokio A bunch of koromiko. It is said that here, near Riverton, moa were killed. Koromiko was the wood traditionally used for cooking moa. The name of the stream has now been changed to Moa Creek.

Puku Named after a woman carried away by the māeroero. Literally, belly.

Pukurahi *puku* (belly); *rahi* (big). Big belly.

Pukutahi Named for a chief who was killed at Lake Te Anau. Literally, *puku* (belly); *tahi* (single).

Punakāiki *puna* (a spring); *kāiki* (a misspelling of *kāike* or *kāika*: to lie in a heap). This is the site of the famous 'Pancake Rocks', which lie in heaps, and the 'spring' is no doubt the blow-hole. But there was a Ngāi-Tahu belief that Punakāiki is a word that describes the neck and throat of a human being, the rock and blow-holes being likened to them.

Punakāiki rocks, West Coast.

Punakītere Swiftly flowing spring.

Punapito *puna* (spring); *pito* (end). End of the spring.

Punaruku *puna* (spring); *ruku* (to sink or dive). To sink into a spring. The name has been brought from Hawaiki.

Punganui A corrupt form of Ponganui, a large tree-fern.

Pungarehu Ashes.

Puni The encampment, or to be blocked up.

Pūniho Ambush.

Pūniu Fern.

Puniwhakaū *puni* (camp); *whakaū* (to arrive). To reach camp.

Pūponga Hunched up.

Pūpū The largest freshwater spring in the world at Tākaka is sadly misnamed. Properly it was known to the Māori as Waikaremumu, which could be rendered Boisterous wind that ruffled the waters. It was shortened by Pākehā to Mumu and possibly corrupted to Bubu; but the Bubu diggings were some miles away. The name was given to the springs, and it was thought that the original Māori must have been Pupu.

The Pupu Stream in Marlborough is named after a shellfish.

Pupuke The name in full is Pupuke-moana, the overflowing lake.

Pūrakanui Correctly, Pūrākaunui. *Pū* (heap); *rākau* (timber); *nui* (big). Big heap of firewood. The inhabitants of Goat Island were slaughtered in tribal warfare and their bodies put in a great pile like a heap of firewood.

Puramāhoi *pura* (to twinkle or shine); *māhoi* (steadily). To shine steadily.

Pūrangi A bag net for catching lampreys. Such nets were totally enclosed except for a narrow opening, and this place was a clearing in the bush with a similar appearance.

Pūrau A spear or fork. It may have had some connection with a traditional mussel basket.

Pūrēhua A moth.

Pūrekireki Tufts of grass, or a heap of fragments.

Pureora A sacred rite performed for the recovery of the sick.

Purerua *pure* (to set free from tapu); *rua* (two).

Pūrewa To float.

Pūriri Native tree. The place was named because the pūriri grew so plentifully.

Puru Full, or a plug.

Putangahau Possibly a shortened form of Te Putangaotehau, The place where the wind comes from.

Putarepo The place at the end of the swamp where it could be crossed.

Pūtaringamotu The place of the severed ear. It was a figurative expression for an isolated patch of bush, the site of Riccarton.

Putāruru Correctly, Putaāruru. *Puta* (hole, or to appear); *ā* (after the manner of); *ruru* (owl, or morepork). The nest or hole of a morepork, which is often found in a hollow tree.

Pūtiki In full, Pūtiki-whara-nui-a-Tamatea-pōkai-whenua, The place where Tamatea the navigator tied his topknot with flax. Tamatea of the Tākitimu canoe went ashore at Whanganui and had his hair dressed. The slave procured flax, but it was rotten and broke. Tamatea said it was not like the wharanui (a kind of flax) obtained on the East Coast. The place was named after the incident.

Pūtōrino Flute.

Pūwera Warm.

R

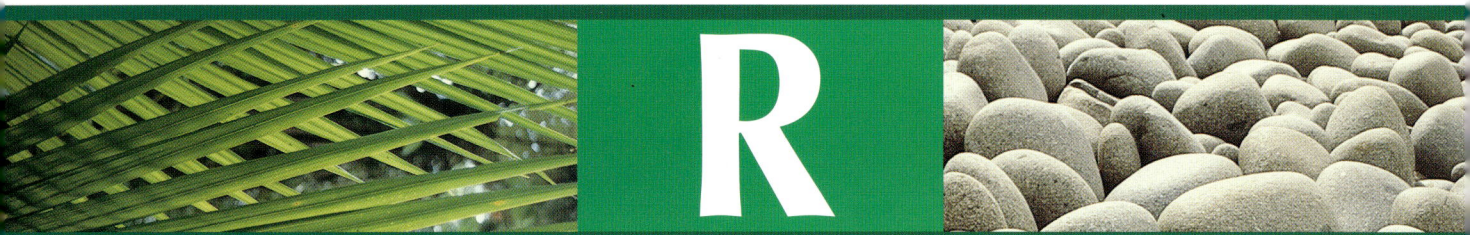

Raetihi *rae* (headland); *tihi* (summit). Prominent summit.

Rāhiri To welcome.

Rāhotu *rā* (sun); *hotu* (to long for). To long for the sun.

Rāhui Boundary post. In full, Pou-rāhui. It also means a sanctuary.

Rai Ribbed, or furrowed. It probably should be *rae* (headland).

Rākaia Adorned. It is probably the South Island form of rāngaia (to arrange in ranks), and refers to the need for strong men to stand in ranks to break the force of the current for the weaker ones when attempting to ford the river.

Rakanui Correctly, Rākaunui. *Rākau* (tree); *nui* (big). Big tree.

Rākau Tree, or timber.

Rākauhauka *rākau* (wood, or tree); *hauka* (South Island form of *haunga*: to smell).

Rākauhaunga See Rakauhauka.

Rākaunui *rākau* (tree); *nui* (big, or many). Big tree, or many trees.

Rākauroa *rākau* (tree); *roa* (long). Tall tree.

Rākautao *rākau* (timber); *tao* (spear). Wood for making spears.

Rakiura *raki* (South Island form of *rangi*: sky); *ura* (glowing). Glowing sky. The Māori name for Stewart Island. There is another tale that a young chief wished to marry but arrived just too late, for the young woman had already wed. The name in full is Te Ura o Te Raki-tāmau, The blushing of Te Raki-tāmau.

Rakiura, or Stewart Island.

Ramaiku Māori form of Damascus.

Ramarama A native tree.

Rānana Māori form of London.

Ranganui *ranga* (parade); *nui* (big). A long line of warriors.

Rangataua A grasshopper; or *ranga* (line of warriors); *taua* (war party). Warriors drawn up in ranks.

Rangatira Chief.

Rangaunu *ranga* (shoal of fish); *unu* (to pull out). Good fishing.

Rangiahua Great; or to approach the sky.

Rangiaowhia *rangi* (sky); *aowhia* (clouded). Clouded sky.

Rangiātea Short for Rangiātea-te-tūāhu-o-Io-mata-kanakana, The shrine of Io of the far-seeing eyes. A sacred name which came from Hawaiki.

Rangiawhia See Rangiaowhia.

Rangihaeata The first rays of morning light.

Rangihoua Named after a chief of long ago.

Rangikura *rangi* (sky); *kura* (red). Red sky. The original name was Whenuakura, red land.

Rangiora Good weather after a bad spell, or an invalid getting better, or day of peace. In the North Island it refers to a shrub.

Rangiotū The day of the god of war.

Rangitoto is a landmark on Auckland's horizon.

Rangipō *rangi* (sky); *pō* (night). The place where the sky is dark, a reference to the time when Ngātoro-i-rangi called down fire on his enemies.

Rangiputa *rangi* (sky); *puta* (to pass through). To cross the sky.

Rangiriri *rangi* (sky); *riri* (angry). The angry sky.

Rangitaikī *rangi* (chief); *tai* (tide); *kī* (full). A great river like a full tide.

Rantitata *rangi* (sky, or day); *tata* (lowering clouds). A day of lowering clouds.

Rangitīkei *rangi* (sky, or day); *tīkei* (to stretch the legs). The day of striding out. It may also refer to a ford which was crossed by walking on tip-toes.

Rangitoto *rangi* (sky, or day); *toto* (blood). A common name in New Zealand, usually imported from Hawaiki. Rangitoto Island, Auckland, is in full Ngā Rangi-i-totongia-a-Tama-te-kapua, The days of the bleeding of Tama-te-kapua. The famous chief of the Arawa canoe was badly wounded here.

Rangitūkia *rangi* (day); *tūkia* (to be attacked). The day of the attack.

Rangiuru *rangi* (sky); *uru* (west). The western sky.

Rangiwāhia *rangi* (sky); *wāhia* (to split). Break, through which the sky can be seen, or a glimpse of heaven. A party of travellers came either to a clearing or to a moment when there was a rift in the clouds.

Rānui *rā* (sun); *nui* (many). Plenty of sunshine. A modern name.

Raorikia Māori form of Laodicea.

Rapahoe Paddle blade.

Rāpaki Kilt. When the chief Te Rangiwhakaputa took possesion, he put down his kilt to mark his ownership.

Rapaura Running waters.

Rāroa *rā* (day); *roa* (long). Named by Ihenga because he spent so many hours paddling his canoe.

Rātā A native tree.

Rātana Named after the Māori prophet.

Rātānui *rātā* (native tree); *nui* (many). Plenty of rātā trees.

Raukawa Leaves of the kawakawa. They were

worn by a chief in mourning and thus gave the name of the Ngāti-Raukawa tribe. Raukawa was the Māori name for Cook Strait.

Raukūmara *rau* (leaf); *kūmara* (sweet potato). Kūmara leaves.

Raumati Summer.

Raupō Native reed.

Raurimu *rau* (many, or leaf); *rimu* (red pine). Many rimu or Rimu leaf.

Rāwene *rā* (day); *wene* (many). Many days.

Rāwhiti The place of the sunrise.

Rāwhitiroa *rā* (sun); *whiti* (to shine); *roa* (long). Long sunshine. It may also mean In the direct line of the sun, as the settlement ran from east to west.

Rēhia Pleasure.

Rehutai Sea spray.

Reikorangi The gate of heaven, or the breast of heaven. A slave of this name was buried here.

Rēinga The underworld.

Cape Rēinga, the leaping-off point where the spirits of the dead reach the underworld.

Remuera Correctly, Remuwera, the burnt edge of a flax garment.

Repo Swamp.

Reporoa *repo* (swamp); *roa* (long). Long swamp.

Rere Waterfall.

Retāruke Correctly, Reretāruke. *Rere* (waterfall); *tāruke* (trap for crayfish).

Rewa To begin, or to meet.

Rewanui *rewa* (mast); *nui* (big). Big mast.

Rewarewa Native tree.

Rikiriki Scattered.

Rimu Red pine.

Rimu trunks.

Rimunui *rimu* (native tree); *nui* (big, or many). Many rimu.

Rimurapa *rimu* (seaweed); *rapa* (to look for). The Māori name for Sinclair Head.

Rimutaka Correctly, Remutaka, to sit down to rest. It refers to an incident when Hau was pursuing his wife.

Rīpa Correctly, Ripapa. *Rī* (flax rope); *papa* (flat rock). A canoe was tied by a flax rope to a rock on the island.

Riponui *ripo* (whirlpool); *nui* (big). Big whirlpool.

Riwaka Correctly, Riuwaka. *Riu* (inside, or bulge); *waka* (canoe). The inside or bulge of a canoe.

Rohepōtae *rohe* (rim); *pōtae* (hat). Rim of the hat, the term applied to the boundary of the King Country after the New Zealand Wars. The Kingite Māori said that it was as if the hat had been taken away, leaving them only the rim.

Romahapa *roma* (stream, or channel); *hapa* (crooked). Crooked channel.

Rona To bind, or swirling.

Rongokōkako *rongo* (to listen); *kōkako* (native crow). Listening to the kōkako. It may be named after the father of Tamatea.

Rongotai *rongo* (sound); *tai* (sea). The sound of the sea. A modern name.

Rongotea Probably named after a chief.

Roto Lake.

Rotoaira *roto* (lake); *a* (of); *Ira* (a person). The lake of Ira.

Rotoakiwa *roto* (lake); *a* (of); *Kiwa* (a person). The lake of Kiwa.

Rotoatara *roto* (lake); *a* (of); *Tara* (a chief). The lake of Tara, who killed the taniwha that inhabited it. The lake is now dried up.

Rotoatua *roto* (lake); *atua* (god). The lake of the god.

Rotoehu *roto* (lake); *ehu* (turbid). Turbid lake.

Rotoiti *roto* (lake); *iti* (little). Little lake. The name of the northern Rotoiti in full was Te Roto-iti-kite-a-Ihenga, The little lake seen or discovered by Ihenga.

Rotokaha *roto* (lake); *kaha* (boundary). The boundary lake.

Rotokākahi *roto* (lake); *kākahi* (freshwater shellfish). The shellfish were killed by the Tarawera eruption. The Green Lake.

Rotokawa *roto* (lake); *kawa* (bitter). Lake of bitter waters.

Rotokawau *roto* (lake); *kawau* (shag). Shag lake.

Rotokohu *roto* (lake); *kohu* (fog or mist). Misty lake.

Rotomā *roto* (lake); *mā* (clear). Lake of clear waters.

Rotomahana *roto* (lake); *mahana* (warm). Warm lake.

Lake Rotomahana.

Rotomakariri *roto* (lake); *makariri* (cold). Cold lake.

Rotomanu *roto* (lake); *manu* (bird). Lake of birds.

Rotongaro *roto* (lake); *ngaro* (lost, or hidden). Hidden lake.

Rotoroa *roto* (lake); *roa* (long). Long lake.

Rotorua *roto* (lake); *rua* (two). The second lake. The full name was Rotorua-nui-a-Kahu. It was the second big lake to be discovered by Ihenga, who named it after his father-in-law Kahu-mata-momoe.

Rototuna *roto* (lake); *tuna* (eel). Eel lake.

Rotowaro *roto* (lake); *waro* (live coals). A fire glowing by the lakeside.

Rotowhero *roto* (lake); *whero* (red). Red lake, so-called because of the iron oxide deposits.

Rotowhio *roto* (lake); *whio* (blue duck). Lake or pool of the blue duck.

Rotu A sleep-making spell.

Ruahine A wise woman, or an old woman.

Ruakākā Nesting place of the parakeets.

Ruakituri *ruaki* (to vomit); *turi* (knee, or post).

Ruakura *rua* (pit); *kura* (red). Pit in the red earth.

Ruakurī *rua* (pit); *kurī* (dog). Cave of the dogs. Wild dogs were found living by the mouth of the cave.

Ruamāhanga *rua* (two); *māhanga* (fork). Twin forks. Hau discovered a drinking trough and a bird-snare in the twin forks of a tree.

Ruamoko *rua* (pit or hole); *moko* (lizard). Home of the lizard.

Ruapehu *rua* (hole); *pehu* (to explode, or make a loud noise). Ruapehu has two vents or blow-holes from which steam is expelled.

Ruapekapeka *rua* (hole); *pekapeka* (native bat). The bat's nest. Thousands of bats lived in the hollows of trees.

Ruapuke *rua* (two); *puke* (hill). Two hills.

Ruaroa *rua* (pit); *roa* (long). Long pit.

Ruatāhuna *rua* (two, or pit); *tāhuna* (sandbank). Two sandbanks.

Ruatangata *rua* (pit); *tangata* (man). Cave in which people lived.

Ruataniwha *rua* (two); *taniwha* (water monster). Two great taniwha once lived in the lake. They fought over a boy who fell in, and their struggles formed the Tukituki and Waipawa Rivers, which drained the lake.

  Other places with this name mean Taniwha pit or cave.

Ruatapu *rua* (pit); *tapu* (sacred). Sacred cave.

Ruatoki *rua* (pit, or two); *toki* (adze). Two adzes, or adze in the cave.

Ruatōria Correctly, Ruaatōria, kūmara pit belonging to Tōria.

Ruawāhia *rua* (pit); *wāhia* (split). Gulch cleft by volcanic action.

Ruawai *rua* (pit, or two); *wai* (water). Water in a cave, or two streams.

Ruawaro *rua* (cave); *waro* (live coals). Embers in a cave.

Rukuhia The act of diving.

Rūnanga An assembly.

Runaruna A plant, or a game.

Ruru Owl or morepork.

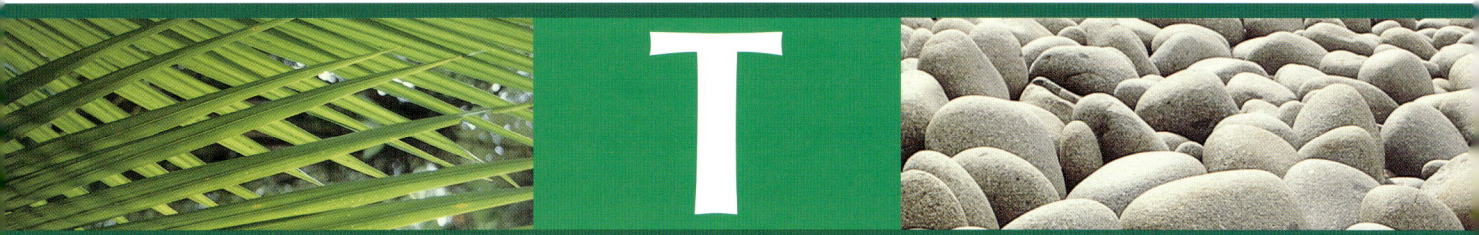

Taemaro *tae* (to dye); *maro* (apron). Dyed apron.

Tahaia *taha* (to pass, on one side); *ia* (current). Passing along the slack water of the stream.

Tahakopa *taha* (side); *kopa* (curved). Curved side.

Tahatika Coastline, or at the edge of the river.

Tahawai *taha* (side); *wai* (sea). Seaside.

Tāheke Waterfall.

Tāhekeaua *tāheke* (waterfall); *aua* (herring). A place for catching herrings by the waterfall.

Tāhekeroa Long river rapid or cataract.

Tahora A clearing, or an expanse of open country.

Tahoraiti Little clearing.

Tahoramaurea Uncultivated, or covered with tussocks.

Tāhuna Sandbank or shoal.

Tāhuna Beach, Nelson.

Tāhunanui *tāhuna* (sandbank); *nui* (many).

Tāhurangi The first Māori to ascend Mount Egmont/Taranaki. Literally, *tāhu* (ridgepole); *rangi* (sky).

Taiamai An old name for the Bay of Islands. In full it is Ka kata ngā pūriri o Taiamai, The pūriri trees of Taiamai are laughing.

Taiaroa Named after the chief Taiaroa.

Taieri Correctly, Taiari, tide on the eleventh night of the moon.

Taihape Originally Ōtaihape, the place of Taihape. Literally, *tai* (angle); *hape* (crooked).

Taiharuru *tai* (sea); *haruru* (resounding). Thundering sea.

Taihoa By and by.

Tāikirau *tāiki* (snag); *rau* (many). Many snags.

Tāiko The name of a Māori, sometimes spelt Tycho. Literally, rib or basket.

Taikōrea *tai* (sea); *kōrea* (small canoe). Small canoe on the sea.

Tainui One of the canoes of the migration. Literally, *tai* (sea); *nui* (big). Great sea.

Taioma White soil.

Taipo Goblin, or devil. The river was given this name because when it was in flood it deserved the name. It is no doubt of modern origin.

Taipoiti Little Taipo.

Taipuha A very high tide.

Tairua *tai* (tide); *rua* (two). Two tides, one from the north and the other from the south.

Taitā Driftwood in the bed of the river.

Taitamāhine *tai* (sea); *tamāhine* (girls). The sea of girls — the peaceful east coast waters, compared with Taitamatāne, the rough west coast, which was called The sea of men, where warriors, not girls, were needed to man the canoes.

Taitamatāne See Taitamāhine.

Taitapu An obsolete word for boundary. Literally, *tai* (tide); *tapu* (sacred).

Taitimu *tai* (tide); *timu* (ebb). Ebb tide.

Takahanga Track or footpath.

Takahē Native bird, the *Notornis*.

Takahiwai *takahi* (to tramp); *wai* (water). To trample into the water.

Takahue *taka* (heap); *hue* (gourd). Heap of gourds.

Takairitawa To jerk out of the water. Thousands of ducks were caught in this way.

Tākaka Bracken. A name that comes from the Society Islands.

Takānini Named after the friendly chief Ihaka Takaanini. Literally, *taka* (heap); *nini* (to glow).

Takapau Flax sleeping mat. A pā in the Far North was given this name because the people of Tainui put down a mat and went to sleep, i.e. they resided there for some time.

Tākapu Gannet.

Takapuna *taka* (assembly); *puna* (spring). The gathering of people who drank at the spring were Tainui men claiming possession of the land.

Takiroa *taki* (sound); *roa* (long). Echo. The name of the rock shelter at Waitaki where there are Māori paintings. There is a very clear echo.

Tākitimu A famous canoe of the migration commanded by Tamatea. It was petrified in the form of the Tākitumu or Tākitimo Mountains.

Takitūī *taki* (to follow); *tūī* (native bird). To follow the tūī.

Takiwā-waiariki *takiwā* (district); *waiariki* (hot springs). A general name for the thermal district.

Takutai *taku* (coast); *tai* (sea). Sea coast.

Tama-ahua The peak on Mount Egmont/Taranaki is named after the first Māori to ascend it.

Tamahere *tama* (son); *here* (tie up).

Tāmaki Battle. The isthmus was tāmaki-whenua, a contested land. It was known as Tāmaki-makau-rau, Tāmaki of a hundred lovers.

Tamarau *tama* (son); *rau* (many). Many sons.

Tāneatua The tohunga (priest) of the Mātaatua canoe. Literally, Tāne the god.

Tāneauroa Named after an old chief. Literally, *tāne* (man); *au* (whirlpool); *roa* (long). The man of the long rapid or whirlpool.

Tānekaha *tāne* (man); *kaha* (strong). Strong man.

Tangahoe Named by Turi after his paddle.

Tangarākau Fallen trees, referring to a great quantity of trees carried down by the river when in flood.

Tangiaro In full, Tangiaro-o-Kahu. *Tangi* (to weep); *aro* (desire for); *o* (of); *Kahu* (Kahu-mata-moemoe). After the death of his father, Kahu-mata-momoe turned his face to Moehau where his father was buried, and chanted a lament of yearning and sorrow.

Tangiihi Correctly, Tangaehe, the noise of the rustling or murmuring tide. There are beds of shells on the foreshore and the waves ripple over them.

Tangimoana *tangi* (lament); *moana* (ocean). The lament of the ocean.

Tangitere *tangi* (to cry or lament); *tere* (swiftly, or to float).

Tangiterōria *tangi* (to cry); *te* (the); *rōria* (conch shell). The sound of the trumpet. Eel weirs were built on the Wairoa River, and as the Māori paddled their canoes up to them the force of the water was audible and was likened to the sound of a conch shell being blown.

Tangiwai *tangi* (to weep or lament); *wai* (water). Weeping waters. Noted for its sudden floods which many years ago were responsible for the death of a chief, and for the terrible railway disaster in 1953. Fiordland greenstone is called tangiwai because of the flecks in it that resemble tears.

Tangoio *tango* (to take hold of); *io* (a strand of rope or lock of hair). To hold a strand of rope.

Tangowahine *tango* (to seize); *wahine* (woman). To abduct a woman.

Taniwha Water monster.

Taonui *tao* (spear); *nui* (big). Great spear.

Taoroa *tao* (spear); *roa* (long). Long spear.

Tapanui Possibly a contraction of Te-tapuwae-o-Uenuku, The footprints of the rainbow god. Or literally, The great edge, referring to the edge of the forest. A third theory is that the name was originally Te Papanui, The great flat area of country.

Tapawera *tapa* (edge); *wera* (hot, or burnt). The burnt fringe (of the forest).

Tapu Sacred. Usually given for a particular reason, as at Coromandel, where the great battle resulted in many dead being buried and making the place sacred; or as at Riwaka, where a tohunga placed a hair of his head near the doorway of his house to keep intruders away.

Cabbage trees on the Coromandel Peninsula near Tapu.

Tapuaeharuru *tapuae* (footsteps); *haruru* (sounding). The noise of footsteps, or resounding footsteps. At Taupō the name was given because of the caverns which caused footsteps to resound. Ihenga gave the name in Northland because of his own footsteps.

Tapuaenuku The footsteps of the rainbow god. In full, Tapuae-Uenuku.

Tapuhi To nurse.

Tāpui Friend, or close companion.

Tapuwae Footsteps, the place in Taranaki named by Turi. Tapuwae, the site of Wairoa Post Office, was named by Sir James Carroll after a chief.

Tapuwaeharuru See Tapuaeharuru.

Tapuwaeroa *tapuwae* (footsteps); *roa* (long). Long footsteps. They were made by the giant Rongokako, who left his footprints at Cape Kidnappers, Māhia, and East Cape.

Tarakai *tara* (sea bird); *kai* (to live). A place where sea birds nested.

Tarakohe *tara* (thorn); *kohe* (native plant).

Taramakau Possibly Teremakau. *Tere* (to flow); *makau* (curve). Another interpretation is that it means *tere* (swift); *makau* (spouse), referring to a man who was in search of his absconding wife who turned to stone.

Taramea Spear-grass.

Taranaki There have been many theories about this name. *Tara* (peak), presents no problems; *naki* may be *ngaki* (clear of vegetation). Probably Taranaki was the tribal name given to the mountain. A very old name was Pukehaupapa, Ice mountain, and when referring to its graceful shape it was called Puke-o-naki.

Tararua *tara* (peak); *rua* (two). Two peaks. The double peaks of the Tararua Range are Pukeamoamo and Pukeahurangi opposite Ōtaki, both named by Rangi-kaikore (Rangi the foodless), because he broke two tara or bird spears while on the range.

Tarata A native tree.

Taratahi *tara* (peak); *tahi* (single). Single peak — in this case Mount Holdsworth.

Tarawera *tara* (bird spear); *wera* (burnt). Hikawera of Hawke's Bay had a successful season killing birds, and left his spears in a hut. When he returned the next season he found that the hut and his spears had been burnt.

Tāreha Ochre.

Tārewa The full name is Tārewa-pounamu. *Tārewa* (to suspend); *pounamu* (greenstone). A greenstone ornament was hung on a tree as a sacred offering.

Tāriki Possibly Tārika, to toss about.

Taringamotu *taringa* (ear); *motu* or *mutu* (cut off). Mutilated ear.

Tārukenga Place of slaughter.

Tātaikoko *tātai* (to adorn); *koko* (pendant). The chief Pawa adorned himself at this place.

Tatara A species of shark.

Tātara-a-kina *tātara* (spine); *a* (of); *kina* (sea urchin). The spines of the sea urchin. An old chief of Taupō compared this mountainous country to the sea urchins of Heretaunga.

Tātaramoa *tātara* (distant); *moa* (large, extinct, flightless bird). Distant moa.

Tatū To be content, or to touch bottom.

Tātuanui *tātua* (girdle); *nui* (big). Large girdle.

Taueru Hanging in clusters.

Tauhara Isolated, alone. The mountain stands alone on the plain.

Tauherenīkau Correctly, Tauwharenīkau, the overhanging nīkau palms. When Hau was travelling in the Wairarapa he discovered a whare whose walls and roof were thatched with nīkau leaves.

Tauhoa To befriend.

Taukitua The further ridge.

Taumarere To fall, or **Taumārere**: a cord passed over the ridgepole of a house. Possibly Taumāriri, tranquil season.

Taumarunui *taumaru* (screen); *nui* (big). Huge screen. When the chief Pehi Taroa was dying, he asked that a screen be erected to shade him from the sun. He died before the work was completed, with the words 'taumaru nui' on his lips.

Taumata Brow of a hill. This is a component of many place names.

Taumatawhakatangihangakōauauotamateapōkai-whenuakitanatahu The brow of the hill where Tamatea who sailed all round the land played his nose flute to his lady love. There are several forms of this firmly established Māori name, reputed to be the longest in the country. Another form, broken into its component parts, is Te Taumata-okiokinga-whakatangihanga-o-te-kōauau-a-Tamatea-pōkai-whenua.

Tauoma Short for Tauomaoma, to race, or strive in running.

Taupaki A loin mat; or a season of fine weather.

Tauparikākā Correctly, Tauparekākā; *taupare* (to blindfold); *kākā* (native parrot). To blindfold a kākā. This was done to decoy kākā, which were fairly tame. It prevented them from flying away.

Taupiri *tau* (ridge of hill); *piri* (to keep close to). It has been rendered, To clasp round the waist.

Taupō Short for Taupō-nui-a-Tia. *Taupō* (shoulder-cloak); *nui* (big); *a* (of); *Tia* (the discoverer of the lake). The great cloak of Tia. Tia slept by the lake, and it has been conjectured that Taupō is a reference to his long sleep at night at that place.

Lake Taupō.

Tauranga A sheltered anchorage, or a resting place for canoes.

Taurangakawau *tauranga* (sheltered place); *kawau* (shag). A resting place for shags.

Tauranga-kohu *tauranga* (resting place); *kohu* (mists). A place where mists linger.

Tauranga-mangō *tauranga* (landing place); *mangō* (shark). Where the sharks were landed. The old name for Shelly Beach.

Tauraroa *taura* (rope); *roa* (long). Long rope.

Taurarua *taura* (rope); *rua* (two). Two ropes. The Māori name for Judges Bay.

Taurewa Having no settled home.

Tauriko A Pākehā-given name. Originally Taurico, standing for Tauranga Rimu Company. It was thought to be a misspelt Māori name and changed to Tauriko.

Taurikura *tauri* (feather ornament); *kura* (red). Ornament of red feathers.

Tautāne *tau* (ridge of a hill); *tāne* (man). Man on the ridge.

Tautoro To stretch forward.

Tautuku To stoop, or to be at a loss.

Tauwharanui *tau* (ridge of a hill); *wharanui* (a species of flax). Flax bushes on the ridge.

Tauwhare To overhang, or a shelter.

Tawa A native tree.

Tawanui *tawa* (native tree); *nui* (many). Plenty of tawa trees.

Tawhai A native tree.

Tāwharanui *tāwhara* (kiekie flowers); *nui* (many). Plenty of kiekie flowers.

Tāwhiti Trap. This was a place where Pawa of the Bay of Plenty set a trap to catch Rongokako, the giant of Kahuranaki.

Tawhiti is a component of many place names, meaning Tahiti, and has been brought from the homeland of the Māori people.

Tawhitinui A forest in Tahiti.

Tāwhiuau Swirling mists.

Tāwirikohukohu Whirling mists. The mountain holds the clouds when the rest of the Tararua Range is clear.

Te Ahi-a-Manono The flames of Manono. The site of part of Lower Hutt, and a name of great antiquity, as it was a description of the burning of a great house on Manono.

Te Ahi-kai-kōura-a-Tama-ki-te-rangi The full name of Kaikōura.

Te Ahi-manawa-a-Te-Kohipipi The full name of the Ahimanawa Range.

Te Ahi-pūpū-a-Ihenga *te* (the); *ahi* (fire); *pūpū* (mussel); *a* (of); *Ihenga* (the explorer). The fire at which mussels were cooked by Ihenga.

Te Ahuahu *te* (the); *ahuahu* (mounds on which kūmara were grown).

Te Ākau *te* (the); *ākau* (rocky coast). The name was given by the tohunga (priest) of the Tainui canoe because it was too rough to land here.

Te Ako-o-te-tūī-a-Tamaoho The teaching of Tamaoho's tūī bird. It was by a waterfall on the Whangamarino stream. Tūī were taught to speak, usually by a waterfall where there was no other sound to disturb the sound of the teacher's voice.

Te Anahawea *te* (the); *ana* (cave); *Hawea* (the Hawea tribe). Smoke was seen coming from this cave in Bligh Sound in 1842, but the inhabitants of the 'lost tribe' fled. Subsequently this name was applied to the sound.

Te Anahīnātore *te* (the); *ana* (cave); *hīnātore* (phosphorescent). This is the famous rediscovered glow-worm cave of Te Anau, named Te Ana-au.

Te Anau A much disputed name. The following are some of the explanations given: To move to and fro as reeds in a lake; named after a Waitaha chieftainess; The rain on the water; The uneven surface; The long view; The lake of many arms; Water current in a cave. It seems most likely that it was named after Te Anau, the daughter of Hekeia.

Te Anga *te* (the); *anga* (cockleshell, or fruit stone).

Te Ara-a-Hongi Hongi's Track.

Te Ārai *te* (the); *ārai* (screen).

Te Araroa *te* (the); *ara* (path); *roa* (long). The long path. The name was given by the Māori first to the residence of a missionary who had a long path to the front of his house.

Te Arawhata The ladder or bridge. A ravine which gave access to the Panekiri Bluff, Waikaremoana.

Te Aro *te* (the); *aro* (face, or front).

Te Aroha *te* (the); *aroha* (love or affection). Kahu-mata-momoe sat on the summit of this mountain of love, and his heart was filled with affection for the land and people of Te Paeroa-o-Toi, the long range of Toi.

Te Atatū *te* (the); *atatū* (dawn).

Te Au The cloud or fog, the site of the town belt in Dunedin.

Te Aumiti *te* (the); *au* (current); *miti* (swallowed up). The Māori name for French Pass, which in legend was formed by a cormorant.

Te Aunuiotonga *te* (the); *au* (current); *nui* (great); *o* (of); *tonga* (south). The Manawatū Gorge through which the south winds blow.

Te Aute *te* (the); *aute* (paper mulberry tree). The name commemorates an unsuccessful attempt to grow this tropical tree, which is so important to the Polynesians.

Te Awa *te* (the); *awa* (river, or channel).

Te Awaiti *te* (the); *awa* (river, or channel); *iti* (little). The little channel.

Te Awamutu *te* (the); *awa* (river); *mutu* (cut short, or ended). The river above this point was blocked by snags and was unsuitable for canoes.

Te Hana *te* (the); *hana* (glow).

Te Hāpara *te* (the); *hāpara* (spade).

Te Hāroto *te* (the); *hāroto* (pool).

Te Heuheu *te* (the); *heuheu* (brushwood). The body of a famous chief was buried near Lake Taupō, and it was difficult to find at a later date because of the brushwood that had grown over it. The high chief Tūkino had a son, who was named Te Heuheu from this event, and the highest peak of Mount Tongariro bears his name.

Te Hīnau *te* (the); *hīnau* (native tree).

Te Hoe Short for Hoe-o-Tainui.

Te Hoiere Named after a canoe, it is the Māori name for Pelorus Sound.

Te Hope *te* (the); *hope* (waist). This river crossing was waist deep.

Te Horo *te* (the); *horo* (landslide). A descriptive name.

Te Huria *te* (the); *Huria* (Māori form of Judea).

Te Ika-a-Māui *te* (the); *ika* (fish); *a* (of); *Māui* (the discoverer of New Zealand). The North Island was his fish which he pulled up from the depths of the ocean.

Te Ika-a-Parehika The fish of Parehika. The Māori name of Lawyers Head, Dunedin, which legend says was a fish which Parehika pulled from the sea.

Te Ika-a-Poutini The fish of Poutini. An ancient name for the West Coast. Traditionally greenstone was the fish of Poutini.

Te Ika-a-Whataroa *te* (the); *ika* (fish); *a* (of); *whata* (storehouse); *roa* (long). The long fish storehouse.

Te Kaha *te* (the); *kaha* (rope, or boundary line).

Te Kairanga The place where much food is gathered. Forest, river and lagoon teemed with birds and fish, and the land was suitable for cultivation. The Māori name for Linton Military Camp.

Te Kākaho *te* (the); *kākaho* (toetoe or plume-grass).

Te Kākāpō *te* (the); *kākāpō* (ground parrot). Kahu's dog caught a kākāpō here.

Te Kaminaru Correctly, Te Ika-a-Maru, the fish of Maru.

Te Kao *te* (the); *kao* (dried kūmara).

Tekapō Correctly, Takapō. *Taka* (a floor mat); *pō* (night). An exploring party was surprised and frightened at night; they hastily rolled up their sleeping mats and made their departure.

The rugged West Coast coastline, Te Ika-a-Poutini.

Te Karaka *te* (the); *karaka* (native tree).

Te Kauanga-a-Hatupatu *te* (the); *kauanga* (swimming); *a* (of); *Hatupatu* (the young man of Rotorua who dived into the lake and swam underwater to Mokoia Island).

Lake Tekapō.

Te Kaukaroa In full, Te Kaukaharoa. *Te* (the); *kaukaha* (to swim strongly); *roa* (long). The long, strong swimming of Hikaroa, who swam across lake Te Anau at its widest part.

Te Kauwhata *te* (the); *kau* (empty); *whata* (storehouse).

Te Kawa *te* (the); *kawa* (shrub).

Te Kawakawa *te* (the); *kawakawa* (native tree). The daughters of Kupe made a wreath of the leaves of kawakawa, and this place later became Cape Palliser. Several places with this name were remembered as place names from Hawaiki.

Te Kiri *te* (the); *kiri* (short for *kirikiri*: gravel).

Te Kiteroa *te* (the); *kite* (to see); *roa* (long). The long view.

Te Kōhaka pouākai *te* (the); *kōhaka* (South Island form of *kohanga*: nest); *pouākai* (fabulous gigantic bird).

Te Kupenga-a-Taramainuku, Hauraki Gulf from Devonport, Auckland.

Te Kōhanga *te* (the); *kōhanga* (nest).

Te Kopi *te* (the); *kopi* (meeting of streams).

Te Kōpuru *te* (the); *kōpuru* (heavy clouds).

Te Kōroa *te* (the); *kōroa* (finger).

Te Kōura *te* (the); *kōura* (crayfish).

Te Kōwhai *te* (the); *kōwhai* (flowering tree).

Te Kūiti A contraction of Te Kūititanga, the narrowing in. A reference to the confiscation of Māori property after the Waikato War, and also to the constriction of the valley of the Mangaokewa at this point.

Te Kūmara *te* (the); *kūmara* (sweet potato). The site of old kūmara plantations.

Te Kumi *te* (the); *kumi* (fabulous creature or monster).

Te Kupenga-a-Taramainuku *te* (the); *kupenga* (fishing net); *a* (of); *Taramainuku* (a chief). Taramainuku cast his net across the Hauraki Gulf from Cape Colville to Whangarei Heads. The Watchman was one of the centre posts of the net, and the Hen and Chicken Islands the corks.

Te Kupenga-o-Kupe *te* (the); *kupenga* (fishing net); *o* (of); *Kupe* (the famous explorer).

Te Kūrae-o-Tura The headland of Tura, the Māori name for the Devonport foreshore.

Te Kūraetanga-o-te-ihu-o-hei *te* (the); *kūraetanga* (outward curve); *o* (of); *te* (the); *ihu* (nose); *o* (of); *Hei* (an explorer). The outward curve of Hei's nose, named by Hei as the Arawa canoe passed north to Hauraki. The island is sometimes known as The Chief's Nose.

Te Kurī-a-Pawa *te* (the); *kurī* (dog); *a* (of); *Pawa* (a famous Māori chief). Later renamed Young Nick's Head by Captain Cook.

Te Māhia *te* (the); *māhia* (indistinct sound).

Te Māika *te* (the); *māika* (basket of cooked food).

Te Maire *te* (the); *maire* (native tree).

Te Mānia *te* (the); *mānia* (plain).

Te Māpara *te* (the); *māpara* (resin, or comb).

Te Mata *te* (the); *mata* (headland), and many other meanings.

Te Matai *te* (the); *matai* (native tree).

Gannet colony, Cape Kidnappers, Hawke's Bay.

Te Matau-a-Māui The fish-hook of Māui, with which the North Island was hooked. The fish-hook is the great curve of Hawke Bay.

Te Maunga *te* (the); *maunga* (mountain).

Te Maungaroa *te* (the); *maunga* (mountain); *roa* (long).

Te Māwhai *te* (the); *māwhai* (parasitic plant).

Te Mira *te* (the); *mira* (Māori form of mill). A flour mill once stood here.

Te Miro *te* (the); *miro* (native tree).

Te Motu-tapu-a-Tinirau *te* (the); *motu* (island); *tapu* (sacred); *a* (of); *Tinirau* (a legendary chief). The sacred island of Tinirau. An ancient name for Mokoia Island.

Temuka Correctly, Te-umu-kaha. *Te* (the); *umu* (earth oven); *kaha* (strong). The fierce umu. Another meaning given to the name is Strong current, umu here meaning current.

Te Namu *te* (the); *namu* (sandfly). Such names were usually given because of the presence of sandflies.

Te Ngae *te* (the); *ngae* (swamp).

Tengawai Probably a corruption of Te Anawai. *Te* (the); *ana* (cave); *wai* (water). The water cavern.

Te Ngāwhā *te* (the); *ngāwhā* (sulphurous springs). A descriptive name.

Te Ngutu-o-te-manu *te* (the); *ngutu* (beak); *o* (of); *te* (the); *manu* (bird). The beak of the bird.

Te Niho-o-te-kiore *te* (the); *niho* (tooth); *o* (of); *te* (the); *kiore* (rat). Rats' teeth. From an expression of Ihenga's wife when he brought home a bundle of rats and she saw their teeth.

Te Pahū *te* (the); *pahū* (gong). A stone or piece of wood which was struck to summon the people.

Te Paki *te* (the); *paki* (fine weather), and other meanings.

Te Papa *te* (the); *papa* (flat land). A descriptive name.

Te Pāpapa *te* (the); *pāpapa* (calabash). At one time known locally as Pumpkin Flat, which could be said to be a rough translation of the name.

Te Papatapu *te* (the); *papa* (flat); *tapu* (sacred). The sacred flat.

Te Pari *te* (the); *pari* (precipice). A descriptive name for Sheerdown Mountain, Milford Sound.

Tēpene Māori form of the name of a missionary, Stephenson.

Te Pirita *te* (the); *pirita* (supplejack).

Te Pōhue *te* (the); *pōhue* (climbing plant such as convolvulus, clematis, etc.)

Te Poi *te* (the); *poi* (ball).

Te Pokohiwi *te* (the); *pokohiwi* (shoulder). The Māori name for Boulder Bank.

Te Puapua-o-hine-nui-te-pō The entrance to the goddess of death. The fumarole which is now known as the Brain Pot at Whakarewarewa.

Te Puia Geyser, or hot spring.

Te Puka-a-Māui *te* (the); *puka* (South Island form of *punga*: anchor stone); *a* (of); *Māui* (the great explorer). The Māori name for Stewart Island.

Te Puke *te* (the); *puke* (hill).

Te Puna *te* (the); *puna* (spring).

Te Puna-a-Tūhoe The springs of Tūhoe, the Māori name for Fairy Springs.

Te Puninga *te* (the); *puninga* (camping place).

Te Purotu Handsome. One old chief said to another, 'Te purotu o te wahine!' ('What a beautiful wife you have!') and from this the place received its name.

Te Rā *te* (the); *rā* (sun). The Māori name for Daggs Sound, which opens up well to the sun.

Te Ranga-o-Taikehu *te* (the); *ranga* (sandspit); *o* (of); *Taikehu* (a member of the crew of Tainui who swam from this sandspit to the shore at Devonport). A fishing bank is also similarly named.

Tērāpātiki *tērā* (that); *pātiki* (flounder, fish).

Te Rauamoa Probably Te Rauhamoa. *Te* (the); *rauhamoa* (extinct bird).

Te Rawa *te* (the); *rawa* (property, or the cause of a quarrel).

Terawhiti Correctly, Tarawhiti, near to the sunrise, or disturbed crossing.

Te Rēinga The leaping place of spirits. Wairua (souls) lowered themselves from a branch of a pohutukawa at Te Rēinga into the underworld below the kelp.

Te Rere *te* (the); *rere* (leap). Rere, rerenga, and rereka, all with the same meaning, are components of many place names, often recording some famous leap such as that of Hihi, who leaped hundreds of feet to escape his enemies. His fall was broken by trees, and the place named Te Rere-a-Hihi.

Te Rerengawairua *te* (the); *rerenga* (leaping); *wairua* (soul). The leaping place of souls. See also Te Rēinga.

Te Rērewa *te* (the); *rērewa* (Māori form of devil). A name given to a supposedly wicked man by missionary Māori.

Te Rore *te* (the); *rore* (snare).

Te Roto *te* (the); *roto* (lake). A component of many names.

Te Rou *te* (the); *rou* (fowler). The name given because the postmaster was called Fowler.

Te Rua *te* (the); *rua* (pit). A component of several names.

Te Ruahine *te* (the); *ruahine* (old or wise woman).

Te Tao-o-Kupe The spear of Kupe. The Māori name for Jackson's Head where Kupe attempted to cast a spear across Cook Strait.

Te Tātua *te* (the); *tātua* (girdle). Māori name for Three Kings, Auckland.

Te Taumanu-o-te-waka-a-Māui The thwart of Māui's canoe at Kaikōura.

Te Taumata See under Taumata.

Te Tawa *te* (the); *tawa* (native tree). At Te Tawa, Rotorua, Ihenga pushed his canoe with a piece of tawa wood. It stuck in the ground and he left it there, naming the place after it.

Te Teko *te* (the); *teko* (rock).

Pounamu, or greenstone, is highly prized by Māori.

Te Tī *te* (the); *tī* (cabbage tree).

Te Tipua *te* (the); *tipua* (goblin).

Te Tō *te* (the); *tō* (hauling up place). The Māori name for Freemans Bay, Auckland.

Te Tou-o-te-Mātenga The sitting place of Marsden. A place where the Reverend Samuel Marsden sat to talk to the Māori.

Te Tua *te* (the); *tua* (other side, or days gone by).

Te Tūāhu-a-Tuameke-te-ahi-Tāpoa-i-taona-ai-te-manawa-o-Taiapua The sacred place of Tuameke, the fire of witchcraft incantation in which the heart of Taiapua was cooked. Between the Green and Blue Lakes, Rotorua.

Te Uku *te* (the); *uku* (white clay).

Te Umu *te* (the); *umu* (earth oven). A component of many place names.

Te Waewae *te* (the); *waewae* (leg, foot, or footprint).

Tewāhi *te* (the); *wāhi* (place). A component of several names.

Te Wai *te* (the); *wai* (water, or stream). A common component of place names, usually followed by a personal name, or name of a plant or tree.

Te Wai Pounamu An old name for the South Island, The water of greenstone. It should really be Te Wāhi Pounamu, The place of greenstone.

Te Waitere *te* (the); *wai* (water); *tere* (swiftly flowing). The place was named in 1905, partly because of its meaning and partly in memory of the Reverend John Whitely, as it is the Māori pronunciation of his name.

Te Waka-a-Māui The canoe of Māui, from which he fished up the North Island. An old name for the South Island.

Te Weka *te* (the); *weka* (wood-hen).

Te Wera *te* (the); *wera* (heat, or burning).

Te Wētā *te* (the); *wētā* (large native insect).

Te Whāiti *te* (the); *whāiti* (narrow gorge). The full name is Te Whaiti-nui-a-Toi, The great canyon of Toi.

Te Whakaraupō *te* (the); *whaka* (South Island form of *whanga*: harbour); *raupō* (reed). Harbour of the raupō reed, the Māori name for Lyttelton Harbour.

Te Whanganui-a-Tara *te* (the); *whanganui* (great harbour); *a* (of); *Tara* (ancestor of the Ngāi-Tara). The great harbour of Tara, now Wellington Harbour or Port Nicholson. However, it seems more likely that the meaning was The great waiting of Tara, who waited to take revenge on enemies who had killed and eaten his dog.

Te Whata *te* (the); *whata* (food storehouse). Ihenga raised a food-store here.

Te Whetū *te* (the); *whetū* (star).

Tīhaka

Tīhaka A kind of basket.

Tikinui *tiki* (carved figure in wood or greenstone); *nui* (big). Large tiki.

Tikitapu *tiki* (image); *tapu* (sacred). A young woman lost a greenstone tiki while she was bathing in the lake. The Māori name for the Blue Lake.

Tikitere A contraction of Taku tiki i tere nei, My youngest daughter has floated away. The young woman jumped into a boiling pool. Tiki is an endearing contraction of pōtiki, last-born.

Tikitiki Girdle, or knot of hair.

Tikokino *tiko* (evacuation of the bowels); *kino* (bad).

Te Whakaraupō, Lyttelton Harbour.

Tikorangi *tiko* (to protrude); *rangi* (sky). The correct Māori name, which means Sky-piercer.

Tikoraurohe The latrine in the bracken fern.

Tīmaru *tī* (cabbage tree); *maru* (shelter). The correct name is probably Te Maru, The place of shelter.

Tīmatanga The beginning, or starting point.

Tinaaruhe *tina* (fixed); *aruhe* (fern-root). To be prevented from eating fern-root.

Tinakori Correctly, Tinakore. *Tina* (Māori form of the word dinner); *kore* (none). No dinner. Māori workmen on the road forgot to take their dinners with them. The hill (properly Ōtari) may have been named after the road.

Tiniroto *tini* (many); *roto* (lake). Many lakes. A modern descriptive name.

Tinopai *tino* (very); *pai* (good).

Tīnui *tī* (cabbage tree); *nui* (many). Many cabbage trees.

Tiori-pātea *tiori* (to hold up to view); *pātea* (clear).

The Māori name for the Haast Pass. A leader of the group of travellers called out that the path was clear.

Te Whanganui-a-Tara, Wellington Harbour.

Tīpapa *tī* (cabbage tree); *papa* (flat). Cabbage tree flat.

Tiraora *tira* (a company of travellers); *ora* (satisfied). The original name of the bay was Tira, but ora was added to distinguish it from Tīrau.

Tiratū Mast of a canoe.

Tīrau *tī* (cabbage tree); *rau* (many). Many cabbage trees.

Tīraumea Many waving cabbage trees.

Tiritiri In full, Tiritiri-matangi. *Tiritiri* (a twig which indicates the position of a kūmara tuber); *matangi* (the warm north-east breeze).

Tirohanga View.

Tirohia Look, or behold.

Tiroiti Circumscribed view.

Tiromoana *tiro* (view); *moana* (ocean). Sea view.

Tironui *tiro* (view); *nui* (great). Great view.

Tiropahī *tiro* (view); *pahī* (a large sea-going canoe with sails). View of a large canoe.

Tiroroa *tiro* (view); *roa* (long). Extensive view.

Tītahi *tī* (cabbage tree); *tahi* (single). A single cabbage tree.

Tītī Mutton-bird.

Titirangi *titi* (long streaks of cloud); *rangi* (sky). Long streaks of cloud in the sky. Or **Tītīrangi**, a species of veronica.

Titiroa Very long streaks of cloud.

Tititea *titi* (peak); *tea* (white). Steep peak of

glistening white. The Māori name for Mount Aspiring.

Tītoki A native tree.

Tītri A corruption of the Pākehā name tea-tree (for mānuka).

Toa Male, brave, or warrior.

The Bay of Islands, or Tokerau.

Toatoa A native tree.

Toetoes (Harbour) Named after a Māori chief, Toitoi or Toetoe.

Toka Rock.

Tokaanu *toka* (stone); *anu* (cold). A cold stone.

Tokakaroro *toka* (rock); *karoro* (seagull). Seagull rock.

Tokanui *toka* (rock); *nui* (many). Plenty of rocks.

Tokarahi *toka* (rock); *rahi* (many). Many rocks, because of the many blocks of limestone.

Tokaroa *toka* (rock); *roa* (long). Long rock.

Tokatoka Rocks upon rocks. A descriptive name for the lava crag above Wairoa.

Tokerau Correctly, Tokarau. *Toka* (rocks); *rau* (hundred, or many). A hundred rocks. The Māori name for the Bay of Islands.

Tokirima *toki* (adze); *rima* (five). Five adzes.

Toko Pole, or to propel.

Tokoiti *toko* (pole); *iti* (small). Little poles. Or possibly, Tokaiti, little rocks.

Tokomaru The canoe which brought Manaia to New Zealand. Literally, *toko* (staff); *maru* (shade or shelter).

Tokoroa *toko* (pole); *roa* (long). Long pole.

Tokotea Correctly, Tokatea. *Toka* (stone); *tea* (white). White rock. Kahu-mata-momoe placed a white rock on a hill in memory of his father, Tama-te-kapua.

Tolaga An obvious corruption of a Māori name. One conjecture is that when Captain Cook recorded the name he pointed to the mainland and asked what the place was called. The Māori may have thought he was asking the name of the wind, and replied Tarakaka, south-west wind. The original name of Tolaga Bay was Uawā.

Tōmoana Named after a chief. Literally, *tō* (to drag); *moana* (ocean).

Tongapōrutu *tonga* (south wind); *pō* (night); *rutu* (to drive into). Driving into a southerly at night. Whātonga's canoe Kurahaupō was running down the west coast of the North Island when it struck a southerly here at nightfall.

Tongariro *tonga* (south wind); *riro* (carried away). When Ngātoro-i-rangi was on the summit and in danger of perishing from the cold, he called to his sisters in Hawaiki for fire. His words were carried on the wings of the south wind. This name was originally applied to the three peaks Tongariro, Ngāuruhoe, and Ruapehu.

Tōpuni Close together, or a black dogskin cloak.

Tōrea Oyster-catcher.

Tōrere Named after a woman who swam ashore from the Tainui canoe. Literally, to hurry, or fall headlong.

Tōtara A native tree. Tōtara in North Otago was so named because it was the only one of its kind in that district. At one time this place was called Tōtaratahi, a single totara.

Tōtaranui *tōtara* (native tree); *nui* (many). Many totara.

Tōwai A native tree.

Tuahiwi *tua* (on the other side); *hiwi* (ridge). On the other side of the ridge.

Tuai Dark.

Tūākau *tū* (to stand); *ākau* (shore or coast). To stand by the shore of the river. There was a commanding view down the Waikato River for some miles from this place.

Tuamarina Correctly, Tuamarino. *Tua* (beyond); *marino* (calm). Clear view from the plains to the hills.

Tōtaranui Bay, Abel Tasman National Park.

Tuapeka *tua* (beyond); *peka* (branch of a river). On the further side of the stream.

Tuatapere A sacred ceremony before a time for amusement. There has been a suggestion that the name should be Tuatapera, Pout of the lips from water being bitter.

Tuatara A native reptile.

Tūhawaiki Named after a famous Māori chief of Ōtago, known as Bloody Jack.

Tūhua Obsidian. Also the Māori name for Mayor Island, named by Toi. It is an extinct volcano and there are large deposits of obsidian.

Tūī Native bird.

Tukituki To demolish, or batter. See under Ruataniwha.

Tūmahu *tū* (wounded); *mahu* (healed). Healed of a wound.

Tūmai *tū* (to stand); *mai* (this way, or towards the person speaking).

Tūmoana *tū* (to stand); *moana* (ocean, or lake). Standing in the lake.

Tuna Eel.

Tunanui *tuna* (eel); *nui* (many). Plenty of eels.

Tuparoa *tupa* (shellfish); *roa* (long). Long shellfish.

Turakina To be felled or thrown down. Hau, when pursuing his wife, named the stream because a tree was lying across it.

Tūranga Standing. It was a stopping place of Toi's canoe, and was the site of the modern Gisborne. It was also known as Tūranga-nui-a-Kiwa. Tūranga-a-Kupe was the stopping place of Kupe, and is now Seatoun in Wellington.

Tūrangārere Correctly, Tūranga-a-rere. *Tūranga* (standing); *a* (of); *rere* (to fly or wave). It was a place where a taua (war party) stood with feathers waving in their hair.

Tūrangi Named after a chief. Literally, *tū* (to stand); *rangi* (sky). To stand in the sky.

Tūrehu Fairies.

Turiroa *turi* (post); *roa* (long). Long post.

Turua Beautiful, referring to the reflections in the river.

Turuturu-mōkai *turuturu* (to set a post in the ground); *mōkai* (slave). A slave was captured on the spot where the post was set in.

Young Nick's Head near Gisborne, Tūranga.

Tūtaekurī *tūtae* (dung); *kurī* (dog).

Tūtaenui *tūtae* (dung); *nui* (big). The Māori name for Marton.

Tūtāmoe *tū* (to rise up); *tāmoe* (flat top). Mountain rising up with a flat top.

Tūtira Row, or file.

Tūtoko Named after a chief. Literally, *tū* (to stand); *toko* (post). To stand up like a post.

Tutukākā *tutu* (a tree in which snares are set); *kākā* (native parrot). The kākā perch.

Tuturau *tutu* (native tree); *rau* (many). Many tutu trees.

Tututawa *tutu* (to steep in water); *tawa* (a native tree). The place where the tawa berries are steeped in water.

U

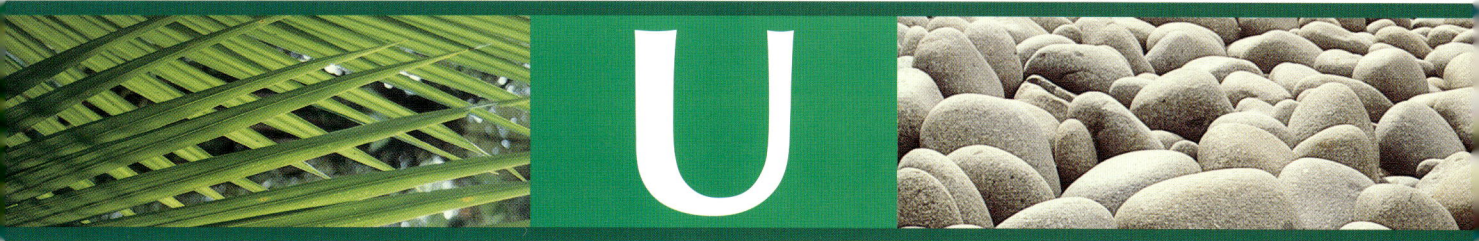

Uawā *ua* (rain); *wā* (season). Rainy season. The original name for Tolaga Bay (see under Tolaga).

Uia To be disentangled.

Umere To keep in time by chanting.

Umukurī *umu* (earth oven); *kurī* (dog). Dog cooked in the umu. What was cooked in the umu was really Kurīmanga, a tohunga (priest).

Umutaoroa *umu* (earth oven); *tao* (to cook); *roa* (long). The umu that took a long time to cook. An incident in Māori history. The site of present-day Dannevirke.

Umutōī *umu* (earth oven); *tōī* (to be moist).

Umuwheke *umu* (earth oven); *wheke* (octopus). Octopus cooked in an umu.

Upoko-ngaro *upoko* (head); *ngaro* (hidden). Hidden head. Ira-ngā-rangi was desolate when her brothers were killed and she died of grief. Lest she be mutilated by enemies, her people cut off her head and hid it in a cave by this stream.

Upoko-pōito *upoko* (head); *pōito* (float). Heads like floats on a fishing net. Some Māori were drowned here, and their heads bobbed up and down like floats on the water. This was near the foreshore at Napier.

Upokororo A freshwater fish.

Urenui Manaia named the river after his son Tū-urenui. Literally, *ure* (figurative expression for courage); *nui* (big). Great courage.

Urewera The name was given almost sarcastically because a chief received a severe burn when he rolled into a fire during sleep.

Urupukapuka *uru* (grove); *pukapuka* (shrub with white leaves). A grove of pukapuka.

Urutī *uru* (grove); *tī* (cabbage tree). A grove of cabbage trees.

Uruwhenua *uru* (west); *whenua* (land). West country.

Utiku A biblical name, Eutychus, in its Māori form. The name was chosen by the chief Pōtaka when he came under missionary influence.

Upoko-pōitu, the Napier foreshore.

W

Waenga In the middle.

Waerenga A clearing.

Waerenga-a-Hika *waerenga* (a clearing); *a* (of); *Hika* (name of a chief). Waerenga's clearing.

Waerenga-o-Kuri *waerenga* (a clearing); *o* (of); *Kuri* (name of a chief). Kuri's clearing.

Waharoa *waha* (mouth); *roa* (long) i.e. the gateway to a palisaded village. Named after the great chief Te Waharoa.

Waianakarua *wai* (water); *ana* (cave); *rua* (two). Water from two caves, or the meeting of waters. Or, the creek of Nakarua.

Waiāniwa Probably a contraction of Waiāniwaniwa.

Waiāniwaniwa *wai* (water); *āniwaniwa* (rainbow, or deep). Deep water, or water where rainbows appear in the spray.

Waiapu *wai* (water); *apu* (to swallow). Swallowing waters. The river is dangerous to cross in time of flood. The rendering may be *waiapu* (a special kind of stone found only in this district, used for polishing adzes).

Waiareka *wai* (water); *reka* (sweet). Sweet or pleasant water.

Waiari *wai* (water); *ari* (clear). Clear water.

Waiariki Hot springs, or curative waters. They are the ariki, chiefs or patriarchs of all water.

Waiaruhe *wai* (water); *aruhe* (fern-root). Stream where the fern-root can be obtained.

Waiatarua *waiata* (song); *rua* (two). Two songs. Or *wai* (water); *atarua* (two images). Double-imaged water. The Māori name for Lake St John, Auckland, now drained.

Waiau *wai* (water); *au* (current). River of swirling currents.

The Waiau River.

Waiaua *wai* (water); *aua* (native fish). Kahu-mata-momoe and Huarere saw the fish in the river and conferred the name.

Waiautoa See Waiauuha.

Waiauuha *wai* (water); *au* (current); *uha* (female). The female Waiau. The male river was Waiautoa (Clarence River). Their sources are close together. In legend they were lovers who drifted apart, and wept for each other.

Waiawa *wai* (water); *awa* (valley). River in the valley.

Waihāhā *wai* (water); *hāhā* (noisy). Noisy water.

Waihao *wai* (water); *hao* (a small eel). Eel river. The name is common. The South Canterbury river was named and discovered by a chief whose wife found these eels particularly acceptable.

Waihapa *wai* (water); *hapa* (crooked). Crooked stream.

Waiharakeke *wai* (water); *harakeke* (flax). Water where the flax grows. At Blenheim the Māori name has been changed to the English equivalent, Flaxbourne.

Waihārara *waiha* (variety of kūmara); *rara* (there).

Waiharuru *wai* (water); *haruru* (resounding). Rumbling or resounding water, descriptive of the sulphur area of Whakarewarewa.

Waihau *wai* (water); *hau* (wind). Windy water.

Waiheke *wai* (water); *heke* (to ebb or drip). Ebbing water.

A bay on Waiheke Island.

Waihemo *wai* (water); *hemo* (to disappear). Disappearing water, referring to the river when the tide has gone out.

Waihī *wai* (water); *hī* (gushing forth). Water gushing out. An old Hawaiki name.

Waihihī Gushing water, a name from Hawaiki.

Waihīnau *wai* (water); *hīnau* (native tree). Hinau trees by the water.

Waihīrere *wai* (water); *hīrere* (to rush). Rushing waters.

Waiho Correctly, Waiau.

Waihōaka *wai* (water); *hōaka* (South Island form of *hōanga*: sandstone). Sandstone stream.

Waihola *wai* (water); *hola* (a rendering of *hora*: spread out). Spreading waters. It is a wide, shallow lake.

Waihopai It should probably be Waiopai, The water of Pai.

Waihopo *wai* (water); *hopo* (to be apprehensive). River that one fears to cross.

Waihora *wai* (water); *hora* (spread out). Wide expanse of water. Lake Ellesmere.

Waihou *wai* (water); *hou* (cold, or new). New or cold river. Probably New river, in the sense that it has cut a new channel.

Waihua *wai* (water); *hua* (fish roe). So named by a Māori because his dog ate a porcupine fish there, but left the roe.

Wai-iti *wai* (water); *iti* (little). Little river.

Waikaia Correctly, Waikea or Waikeha. *Wai* (water); *keha* (burr). The stream where the keha grew. It was named by Rākaihautū because the native burr infested the place.

Waikāka Short for Waikākahi. *Wai* (water); *kākahi* (shellfish). Water where the shellfish may be found.

Waikākaho *wai* (water); *kākaho* (plumes of the toetoe). Toetoe-plume water.

Waikana Short for Waikanakana. *Wai* (water); *kanakana* (lamprey). Lamprey river.

Waikanae *wai* (water); *kanae* (mullet). Hau, who was searching for his wife, looked about out of the corner of his eye (ka ngahae ngā pī), and likened his eyes to the glistening of the mullet.

Waikaraka *wai* (water); *karaka* (native tree). Karaka river.

Waikare *wai* (water); *kare* (to ripple). Rippling water.

Waikareiti *wai* (water); *kare* (to ripple); *iti* (little). Near Lake Waikaremoana.

Waikaremoana *wai* (water); *kare* (to ripple); *moana* (lake). Popularly rendered The sea of rippling waters, but it would be better as The sea of dashing waters, because the waves were agitated by the taniwha who formed the Waikare-tāheke, the raging torrent that runs out of the lake.

Waikāretu *wai* (water); *kāretu* (sweet-scented grass). Kāretu river.

Waikari Ditch or trench. Waikari in Hawke's Bay commemorates Paoa's dog Whakao, who dug (*kari* means to dig) until he found water (*wai*).

Waikato *wai* (water); *kato* (to flow). Full flowing river.

The Waikato River, Hamilton.

Waikaukau *wai* (water); *kaukau* (to bathe). Bathing place.

Waikāura *wai* (water); *kāura* (a form of *kōura*: crayfish). Crayfish were plentiful in this stream.

Waikawa *wai* (water); *kawa* (bitter). Bitter water.

Waikawau *wai* (water); *kawau* (shag). Shag river.

Waikererū *wai* (water); *kererū* (native wood pigeon). Kererū water.

Waikeria *wai* (water); *keria* (dug out). A gouged-out watercourse.

Waikerikeri *wai* (water); *kerikeri* (rushing along violently). The Māori name for the Selwyn River.

Waikēwai Correctly, Waikēkēwai. *Wai* (water); *kēkēwai* (small dragonfly). Dragonfly stream.

Waikiekie *wai* (water); *kiekie* (climbing plant). Kiekie water.

Waikimihia *wai* (water); *kimihia* (sought for). The sought-for water, the Māori name for Hinemoa's Bath on Mokoia Island, to which Hinemoa swam from the mainland and in which she bathed on her arrival.

Waikino *wai* (water); *kino* (bad). Unpleasant water.

Waikite *wai* (water); *kite* (to see). This once-famous geyser at Whakarewarewa could be seen clearly from Rotorua.

Waikiwi *wai* (water); *kiwi* (native flightless bird). Kiwi stream.

Waikōau *wai* (water); *kōau* (shag). Shag river.

Waikohu Mist or fog.

Waikoikoi *wai* (water); *koikoi* (cool). Cool water.

Waikōkopu *wai* (water); *kōkopu* (freshwater fish). Kōkopu stream.

Waikōkōwai *wai* (water); *kōkōwai* (red ochre). Water where red ochre is found.

Waikomiti *wai* (water); *komiti* (mingled). Mingled waters. The Māori name for Glen Eden.

Waikōpua *wai* (water); *kōpua* (deep). Deep water.

Waikorohihī Bubbling or hissing water, a pool at Whakarewarewa.

Waikotūturi *wai* (water); *kotūturi* (kneeling). The water of kneeling. Some defeated warriors were forced to kneel beside the stream with their hands tied behind their backs.

Waikouaiti *wai* (water); *koua*, or *kua* (to become); *iti* (small). The water that decreased. The usual explanation of this name is that the river changed its course, the flow thus decreasing at this point.

Waikōura *wai* (water); *kōura* (crayfish). Crayfish stream.

Waikōwhai *wai* (water); *kōwhai* (flowering tree). Many kōwhai grew here.

Waikumete *wai* (water); *kumete* (wooden bowl). Kumete creek.

Waikuta *wai* (water); *kuta* (a rush). Stream of

rushes. The name was given by Ihenga because of the profuse growth of rushes.

Waimā *wai* (water); *mā* (white). White river. There was a great deal of white limestone in its bed.

Waimaero *wai* (water); *maero* (wild man of the forest). The name is also said to mean deep water channel, or hard water.

Waimāhaka *wai* (water); *māhaka* (South Island form of *māhanga*: twin). Twin waters.

Waimahora *wai* (water); *mahora* (to spread out). Spreading waters.

Waimahuru *wai* (water); *mahuru* (placid). Placid waters. The name was given by Paoa because of the appearance of the stream.

Waimai Probably the original name was Waimatai. *Wai* (water); *matai* (black pine). Black pine river.

Waimakariri *wai* (water); *makariri* (cold). Cold river.

The Waimakariri River.

Waimamaku *wai* (water); *mamaku* (tree-fern). Mamaku stream.

Waimana *wai* (water); *mana* (shrimp). Stream in which shrimps are caught.

Waimanarara *wai* (water); *manarara* (noisy). Turbulent river.

Waimangaroa *wai* (water); *manga* (branch); *roa* (long). Long branch of a river.

Waimangeo *wai* (water); *mangeo* (pungent, mineralised water). The Māori name for Alum Creek.

Waimangu *wai* (water); *mangu* (black). Black water. The name of the famous extinct geyser which threw a huge volume of muddy water high into the air.

Waimanu *wai* (water); *manu* (bird). Stream frequented by birds.

Waimārama *wai* (water); *mārama* (moonlight). Moonlit water. It also means clear water.

Waimarie *wai* (water); *marie* (quiet). Quiet waters.

Waimarino *wai* (water); *marino* (calm, or still). Still waters.

Waimaru *wai* (water); *maru* (sheltered). Calm water.

Waimatā *wai* (water); *matā* (bullet). Stream where bullets are found. A running fight took place there and it is said that bullets may be found in the bed of the stream.

Waimātaitai *wai* (water); *mātaitai* (salty). Brackish water. A descriptive name for a lagoon.

Waimate *wai* (water); *mate* (stagnant). The original name in the South Island was Waimatemate, with the same meaning. Until floods came, the creeks became blocked up and there were many stagnant pools.

Waimatenui *wai* (water); *mate* (stagnant); *nui* (big). Great expanse of stagnant water.

Waimatuku *wai* (water); *matuku* (bittern). Bittern stream.

Waimauku *wai* (water); *mauku* (small fern). A river which when flooded drowned the cabbage trees, so that their tops appeared above the water like small ferns.

Waimaunga *wai* (water); *maunga* (mountain). Mountain stream.

Waimea Several meanings have been given for the name. *Wai* (water); *mea* (unimportant, forgotten). The stream with the forgotten name. Mea may be a contraction of meha (tasteless). The use of the name is widespread, and could mean insipid, tasteless, unimportant, lonely, unpalatable, etc.

Waimeha See Waimea.

Waimiha Probably another form of Waimea, q.v. It may mean Water that is pretty to look at.

Waimihi *wai* (water); *mihi* (to sigh, or regret).

Waimiro *wai* (water); *miro* (native tree). Miro creek.

Waimoari *wai* (water); *moari* (giant swing). The river beside which a moari was erected.

Waimori *wai* (water); *mori* (without tributaries).

Waimotu *wai* (water); *motu* (island). Island stream, or stream with an island in it.

Wainamu *wai* (water); *namu* (sandfly). Stream infested with sandflies.

Waingaro *wai* (water); *ngaro* (lost). Hidden waters.

Waingawa Correctly, Wai-awanga, water of hesitation. Hau hesitated to cross this river when in pursuit of his wife.

Waingongoro *wai* (water); *ngongoro* (gurgling). It also means snoring, and this is the place where Turi snored.

Wainihinihi *wai* (water); *nihinihi* (to glide past). The place where the waters glide past.

Wainono *wai* (water); *nono* (oozing). Oozing water.

Wainui *wai* (water); *nui* (big). Big river.

Wainuiomata *wai* (water); *nui* (big); *o* (of); *Mata* (name of a person). Big stream belonging to Mata.

Waioeka Probably Waioweka. *Wai* (water); *o* (of); *weka* (wood-hen). Weka river.

Waiomatatini The syllables are capable of so many meaningless translations that speculation is idle. It is the place where an ancestor of the Ngāti-Porou tribe was hung up in a pūriri tree, the incident being remembered by the giving of the famous name Tūwhakairiora.

Waiomu *wai* (water); *o* (of); *Mū* (personal name). The water of Mū.

Waione *wai* (water); *one* (beach). Stream on the beach.

Waiongona *wai* (water); *o* (of); *Ngona* (personal name). Water of Ngona.

Waiopani *wai* (water); *o* (of); *pani* (orphan). Orphan water or lake.

Waioraatāne *wai* (water); *ora* (living); *a* (of); *Tāne* (the god of nature). A very famous name in mythology.

Waiorongomai *wai* (water); *o* (of); *Rongomai* (personal name). The water of Rongomai.

Waiotapu Sacred waters.

Waiotemārama *wai* (water); *o* (of); *te* (the); *mārama* (moon). The waters of the moon.

Waiotira *wai* (water); *o* (of); *tira* (sticks set up for purposes of divination). Water of incantation.

Waiotū *wai* (water); *o* (of); *Tū* (the god of war). A pool or stream where ceremonies were rendered to Tū.

Waiouru *wai* (water); *o* (of); *uru* (west). River of the west. The stream is the most westerly branch of the Hautupu River.

Waipā *wai* (water); *pā* (fortified village). River by the pā.

Waipahī *wai* (water); *pahī* (flowing). Flowing water. Actually, The water of Pahi.

Waipango *wai* (water); *pango* (black). Black water.

Waipao *wai* (water); *pao* (to strike). The place was named after Waipao, who was killed by Tūwhakairiora.

Waiapaoa *wai* (water); *paoa* (smoky). Smoky water. In fact it should be called Waiopaoa, the river of Paoa, a famous chief whose people had made a canoe in the forest. He created the river to launch the canoe.

Waipapa *wai* (water); *papa* (flat, or flat rock). Stream across the plain, or stream of the flat rock.

Waipapakauri *wai* (water); *papa* (flat land); *kauri* (native tree). Swampy ground where the kauri grows.

Waipara *wai* (water); *para* (mud). River with a thick muddy sediment.

Waipata *wai* (water); *pata* (dripping). Dripping water.

Waipātiki *wai* (water); *pātiki* (flounder). Water where the flounders may be found.

Waipatukahu *wai* (water); *patu* (to beat); *kahu* (cloak). Water in which garments were beaten.

Waipawa *wai* (water); *pawa* (bird-snare). Waipawa in Hawke's Bay is named after Pawa or Paoa, but has also been rendered Waipawamate, Water smelling strongly, or Dead water.

Waipīata *wai* (water); *pīata* (glistening). Glistening water.

Waipipi *wai* (water); *pipi* (shellfish). Where the pipi are found.

Waipiro *wai* (water); *piro* (stinking). Evil-smelling water.

Waipori Correctly, Waipōuri. *Wai* (water); *pōuri* (dark). Dark river.

Waipoua *wai* (water); *poua* (shellfish). The original name was probably Waipoa, poa being a shellfish found at the mouth of the river. Another conjecture is that the name is **Waipōua**: *wai* (water); *pō* (night); *ua* (rain); water that comes from the rain at night.

The Waipoua forest is known for its stands of mature kauri.

Waipounamu *wai* (water); *pounamu* (greenstone). Greenstone river.

Waipōuri *wai* (water); *pōuri* (dark). Dark stream.

Waipū *wai* (water); *pū* (red). Reddish water. A fairly persistent belief is that *pū* refers to the sound of gunfire.

Waipuku *wai* (water); *puku* (to swell). Swelling water.

Waipukurau *wai* (water); *pukurau* (a large white mushroom). Stream where the mushrooms grow. This is the correct meaning, but it has been conjectured that the name should have been Waipukerau. *Waipuke* (flood); *rau* (many). Many floods.

Wairākei *wai* (water); *rākei* (adorning). The place where the pools were used as mirrors.

Wairaki *wai* (water); *raki* (dry). Dried-up waters. It is the bed of an old lake.

Wairangi Foolish, or excited.

Wairarapa *wai* (water); *rarapa* (glistening). Glistening waters. When Hau saw the beautiful lake and valley his eyes glistened with delight. The glistening is not only of the water but of his eyes.

Wairau *wai* (water); *rau* (many). The plain of a hundred rivers. Simple names like this often have many meanings, and some that have been given for Wairau are, The rift in the clouds, Waters of many streams, and Discoloured waters.

Waireka *wai* (water); *reka* (sweet). Pleasant waters.

Wairepo *wai* (water); *repo* (swamp). Swampy water, or Water running through a swamp.

Wairere Waterfall.

Wairewa *wai* (water); *rewa* (to lift up). Water lifted up. It is the Māori name for Lake Forsyth, the last lake which Rākaihautū scooped out. As the sign that his labours were over, he thrust his kō (digging stick) into the summit of a hill close by, and this was the 'lifting up'.

Wairima *wai* (water); *rima* (five).

Wairio *wai* (water); *rio* (dried up). Dried-up waters. Another conjecture is that the name should be Waireo. *Wai* (water); *reo* (voice). Voice of the waters.

Wairoa *wai* (water); *roa* (long). Usually Long river, but in some places it means High waterfall, and in one case Tall geyser.

Wairongoa *wai* (water); *rongoa* (medicine). Water with curative properties.

Wairongomai Probably the correct form is Waiorongomai, The water of Rongomai.

Wairua Soul or spirit. Or *wai* (water); *rua* (two). Two streams.

Wairuna *wai* (water); *runa* (dock plant). Stream where the dock grows.

Wairunga *wai* (water); *runga* (above, or from above). Stream which flows from the mountains.

Waitaha *wai* (water); *taha* (to pass on one side). Backwater. Some South Island names come from the early Waitaha tribe. Also a name for the Canterbury Plains, an abbreviation of Ngā pākihi-whakateketeka-a-Waitaha, q.v.

Waitahanui *wai* (water); *tahanui* (a variety of cabbage tree). Stream where the cabbage trees grow. Or Big backwater.

Waitahora

Waitahora *wai* (water); *tahora* (spread out, or a small duck). Duck stream, or Spreading waters.

Waitāhuna *wai* (water); *tāhuna* (sandbank). Usually translated Stream of many sandbanks, it was actually named after a Ngāi-Tahu chief.

Waitai *wai* (water); *tai* (tide). Tidal or brackish water.

Waitākaro *wai* (water); *tākaro* (to play or wrestle). Stream running through a games area.

Waitakaruru *wai* (water); *takaruru* (stagnant). Stagnant water. One amusing meaning has been given: *wai* (water); *taka* (to fall); *ruru* (owl). Water that the morepork fell into.

Waitakere *wai* (water); *takere* (deep). Deep pools. Another meaning is Cascading waters. It is thought that the Auckland Waitakere may possibly be a corruption of Waitekauri, Stream where the kauri grows; but it is almost certain that it was named after a chief who was murdered at the mouth of the stream.

The South Island Waitakere (the Nile River) was originally Ngāwaitakerei, The waters of Takerei.

A bush walk in the Waitakere Ranges, Auckland.

Waitaki *wai* (water); *taki* (South Island form of *tangi*: sounding). Rumbling waters, coming from the sound of the river over the shingle beds. There is a legend that the river was formed by the tears of two brothers, whose sister was drowned at the mouth of the river and turned into a rock. The brothers were transformed into two hills near Ohou, and their tears form the river of weeping.

Waitangi *wai* (water); *tangi* (weeping, or sounding). Noisy or weeping waters.

Waitangi.

Waitapu *wai* (water); *tapu* (sacred). Sacred water.

Waitara *wai* (water); *tara* (short for *taranga*: wide steps). River crossed with big steps. Turi forded it with great strides. Another explanation is that it simply means Mountain stream: *tara* (peak); and another that a young man searched for his father by successive throwings of his dart: *whai* (to follow); *tara* (dart).

Waitara on the Mōhaka River is so named because he took with him the bones of his slave to scrape and shape into spears (tara).

Waitārere *wai* (water); *tārere* (to flow copiously). Running streams.

Waitāria *wai* (water); *tāria* (to wait for). Water that has been waited for.

Waitata *wai* (water); *tata* (close). Nearby water.

Waitati The correct name is Waitētē. *Wai* (water); *tētē* (blue duck). Water frequented by blue ducks.

Waitematā *wai* (water); *te* (the); *matā* (short for *matā-tūhua*: obsidian). Water as smooth as the surface of obsidian. It may be a coincidence that the name of the upper reaches of the harbour was Waitīmata, *tīmata* (to begin), being a rock which was a tribal boundary.

Waitematamata *wai* (water); *te* (the); *Matamata* (a taniwha who lived in the creek).

Waitepeka *wai* (water); *te* (the); *peka* (branch). Tributary of the river.

Waitemata Harbour.

e**Waitētē** *wai* (water); *tētē* (dripping). Water dripping from the ground.

Waitetī *wai* (water); *te* (the); *tī* (cabbage tree). Cabbage tree stream.

Waitetuna *wai* (water); *te* (the); *tuna* (eel). Creek where the eels are caught.

Waitoa *wai* (water); *toa* (rough). Rough water.

Waitoetoe *wai* (water); *toetoe* (plume-grass). Toetoe stream.

Waitohi There are three possible explanations for the original name for Picton. It may be a stream where the waitohi baptismal rite was performed. It may be, in full, Te Wera-o-Waitohi, the burning of Waitohi. Waitohi, the sister of Te Rauparaha, is reputed to have been burnt to death in a scrub fire. Or it is the clearing burnt by Waitohi to make a plantation.

Waitohu *wai* (water); *tohu* (to point out). Water that showed the way to two fugitives who escaped to the hills.

Waitomo *wai* (water); *tomo* (shaft). Water entering the cave by means of long shafts.

Waitōtara *wai* (water); *tōtara* (native tree). River where the tōtara trees were plentiful.

Waitoto *wai* (water); *toto* (blood). Probably the scene of a battle.

Waitūī *wai* (water); *tūī* (native bird). Tūī bay or river.

Waituna *wai* (water); *tuna* (eel). Eel stream. It is possible that Waituna West received its Māori name because of an orator who lived there. Some eels remain small and immature, and the Māori ideal of oratory was a flow of words of even length.

Waiuku *wai* (water); *uku* (white clay). A high-born woman came here to choose a husband. The first chief presented was good-looking, but did not impress the woman. His brother who was in the kūmara plantation was hurriedly summoned and scrubbed with white clay from the stream to make him presentable. The uku was known as Māori soap. The story had a happy ending, and the event is commemorated in the name Waiuku.

Waiuta *wai* (water); *uta* (inland). Inland water. Or to load a canoe on the river.

Glow-worm caves, Waitomo.

Waiwera *wai* (water); *wera* (hot). Hot water. The Auckland Waiwera is the site of hot springs. The southern Waiwera is named after Waiwhero, a chief.

Waiwhero *wai* (water); *whero* (red). Red water.

Waiwhetū *wai* (water); *whetū* (star). Star-reflecting water.

Waiwhio *wai* (water); *whio* (blue mountain duck, or whistling duck). Stream of the mountain duck.

fn95

Wakamarino *waka* (South Island form of *whanga*: harbour); *marino* (peaceful). A peaceful bay.

Wakanui *waka* (canoe); *nui* (big). Large canoe.

Wakapatu Correctly, Whakapatu, to strike, or to kill.

Wakapuaka Correctly, Whakapuaka, the name of Kupe's fishing ground in Tahiti, transferred to Nelson. Literally, *waka* (canoe); *puaka* (dry twigs). The early settlers called it Hoke-poke.

Wakarara *waka* (canoe); *rara* (to be thrown broadside on). A canoe thrown on its beam ends.

Wakāri Correctly, Whakaari, to show, or expose to view.

Wakatahuri *waka* (canoe); *tahuri* (overturned). The overturned canoe.

Wakatipu Short for Waka-tipua-wai-māori. Wakatipu is said to be Wakatipua: *waka* (canoe); *tipua* (goblin or monster); *wai māori* (fresh water). The lake was the trough in which the tipua rests, his breathing causing the rise and fall of the lake waters. On the other hand, the original form may be Whakatipu, which means to create or cause to grow, so named because the remnants of defeated tribes retired here to rear their families and build up their strength.

Lake McKerrow is Waka-tipua-wai-tai: *wai-tai* (salt water).

TSS *Earnslaw* on Lake Wakatipu.

Wakatū *waka* (canoe); *tū* (to pile up). The place where broken canoes were dumped. It is the old name for Nelson.

Wānaka Possibly it should be Wānanga, sacred knowledge. Another explanation is that it is Ōanaka (which has much the same sound): *ō* (the place of); *Anaka* (name of a person).

Wangaehu See Whangaehu.

Wanganui See Whanganui.

Whakaari, White Island.

Wangapeka *wanga* (properly *whanga*: harbour or valley); *peka* (edible fern-root). Valley of the fern-root.

Waotū In full, He Wao-tūtahi-ngā-rākau, The place of high trees standing by themselves.

Warea To be absorbed, or to be made unconscious. Possibly named after the wife of Manaia.

Warepā Correctly, Wharepā, fortified house.

Waro A deep pit, or a recess in the rocks.

Weka Wood-hen.

Wekakura *weka* (wood-hen); *kura* (red). Reddish-coloured weka.

Weraroa *wera* (burnt); *roa* (long). Long burn, in preparation for a clearing.

Whaingāroa *whai* (stingray); *ngā* (the); *roa* (long). The Māori name for Raglan Harbour.

Whakaangiangi To make thin.

Whakaari To make visible. The Māori name for White Island, among other places.

Whakahoro To scatter, or to take to pieces.

Whakairi To hang up.

Whakakī To fill. This referred to the lagoon which the Māori liked to see at a high level for fishing and eeling.

Whakakitenga A place where an extensive view can be obtained.

Whakamahi Correctly Whakamahia. Made to work. Several men were forced to work in the cultivations there and were fed with human flesh.

Whakamārama To illuminate, or to explain.

Whakamarino To make peaceful.

Whakapara To make a clearing in the forest.

Whakapoungākau *whakapou* (to establish firmly); *ngākau* (heart). The hills of heart's desire. Tānewhakarara went to hunt in these hills and did not return. His sisters named the range because of the longing their brother had for them, and before they returned to Hawaiki they made hot springs at Tikitere so that their brother could bathe there if he returned.

Whakarewa To cause something to float.

Whakarewarewa The full name is Te Whakarewarewatanga-o-te-Ope-a-Wāhiao, The uprising of the war party at Wāhiao. A war party assembled at the geyser area and performed a war dance before going into action.

Whakarongo To listen, or to inform.

Whakataki To go in search of, or to begin a speech.

Whakatāne To play the man. Wairaka, the daughter of the chief Toroa, jumped ashore from the Mātaatua canoe when it was in difficulties, and took a line ashore. Her famous saying on this occasion was, 'Me whakatāne au i au' ('I shall act like a man'). There are several variations of the story.

Whakatete Disputed ground. A recent name applied to the sacred places where gold prospectors in the Coromandel Peninsula were not permitted to dig.

Whakatiti A leaf used to let the spirit of a dying man escape.

Wall mural, Whakatāne.

Whakatū To stand up, or to make a speech.

Whakatutu To place an object so that water falls onto it, to hold open a basket, or to fasten a net to a hoop.

Whananaki *whana* (to rush); *naki* (steadily). A steady rush (of water).

Whanawhana To bend backwards and forwards.

Whangaehu *whanga* (harbour); *ehu* (turbid). Ehu also means to bail out, and it is said that when Hau crossed this river, he had to bail out his canoe; or that he splashed the water with the flat of his taiaha.

Whangakōkō *whanga* (harbour); *kōkō* (a name for the tūī). Tūī harbour.

Whangamatā *whanga* (harbour); *matā* (obsidian). Obsidian is washed ashore here from Mayor Island.

Whangamoa *whanga* (harbour); *moa* (large, extinct, flightless bird). Moa haven.

Whangamōmona *whanga* (valley); *mōmona* (fat). Fertile valley. There is also a story that a man named Hoti waylaid travellers and killed and ate the plump ones.

Whanganui *whanga* (harbour); *nui* (big). Great harbour. The Māori pronunciation in this district is different from that in other parts, especially because w is substituted for wh. For this reason the form Wanganui became the accepted spelling, although the river now takes the form Whanganui.

Whanganui-o-Hei The great bay of Hei. The Māori name for Mercury Harbour.

Whangapara *whanga* (harbour); *para* (sediment). Muddy harbour.

Whanganui.

Whangaparāoa *whanga* (harbour); *parāoa* (whale). Whale harbour. This is the place where canoes of the great migration landed. A whale was stranded on the beach and became an object of dispute between the men of the Tainui and Arawa canoes.

Whangapē It is said that the name means Waiting for the inside of the paua. The name comes from the Society Islands.

Whangapipiro Evil-smelling place. This was the hot spring in which the bird-ogress who chased Hatupatu was killed.

Whangapoua *whanga* (harbour); *poua* (shellfish). Harbour of shellfish.

Whangarā *whanga* (harbour); *rā* (sun). Sunny bay. The name was brought from Rarotonga.

Whangarae *whanga* (harbour); *rae* (headland). The bay of many capes, the Māori name for Croisilles Harbour.

Whangarātā *whanga* (harbour); *rātā* (native tree). Bay of rātā trees.

Whangarei *whanga* (harbour); *rei* (cherished possession). It probably means The waiting of Rei. A young woman, Reipae, from Waikato, waited here for her lover, but grew tired and married another young man. Her sister Reitū married the rejected lover.

Whangarei Harbour.

Whangaroa *whanga* (harbour); *roa* (long).

Whangaruru *whanga* (harbour); *ruru* (sheltered). Sheltered harbour.

Whangateau *whanga* (harbour); *te* (the); *au* (current). The harbour with the strong current.

Whangatoetoe *whanga* (harbour); *toetoe* (plume-grass). Toetoe bay.

Whare House. The name is usually given by Pākehā, as in Whare Flat.

Whareātea *whare* (house); *ātea* (space, or out of the way). A large house to accommodate everyone. Such a house stood here for the entertainment of guests long ago.

Wharehine *whare* (house); *hine* (young woman). The house of girls.

Wharehuia *whare* (house); *huia* (extinct native bird). Home of the huia.

Wharehunga *whare* (house); *hunga* (company of people). A large house in which to accommodate people.

Whangaroa Harbour.

Wharekōpae House with a door at the side (an unusual place for the door).

Wharekurī Correctly, Te Warokurī, the chasm of the dog.

Wharemā whare (house); mā (free from tapu). Common house.

Wharemauku whare (house); mauku (fern). House built of fern-trees.

Wharenui A variety of flax.

Whareorino whare (house); o (of); rino (iron). Corrugated iron house.

Wharepāina whare (house); pāina (to warm oneself). It has been suggested that as it is in a region of pine plantations, paina stands for pine. The house in the pines.

Wharepapa whare (house); papa (flat land). House on the flat.

Wharepoa whare (house); poa (sacred food). House of sacred food.

Whareponga whare (house); ponga (tree-fern). Tree-fern house.

Wharerākau whare (house); rākau (timber, or tree). House of timber, or house among the trees.

Wharerātā whare (house); rātā (native tree). House among the rātā.

Whareroa whare (house); roa (long). Long house.

Wharetoa whare (house); toa (warriors). House of men.

Wharetōtara whare (house); tōtara (native tree). The house made of tōtara bark.

Wharetukura whare (house); tukura (a species of fern-tree). Fern-tree house.

Whataarama whata (food-store); a (of); Rama (name of a man). The food-store of Rama, the Māori name for the Torlesse Range as well as a peak in the Southern Alps.

Whatamongo Correctly, Whatamangō; whata (food-store); mangō (shark). Storehouse for shark flesh.

Whataroa whata (storehouse); roa (long). Long storehouse.

Whatatutu whata (storehouse); tutu (shrub). Storehouse near the tutu bushes.

Whatawhata Elevated food-store.

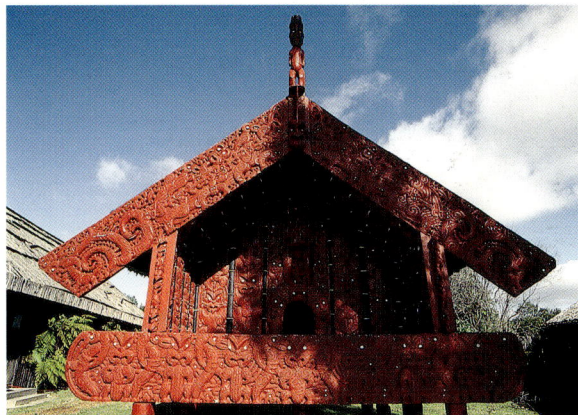

A traditional Māori food-store. They were built on stilts to keep the contents dry and safe.

Whatitiri Thunder. Ihenga chanted a karakia on the hill, and the thunder roared as the chant ended.

Whātoro To stretch out, or to thrust forward.

Whau A native tree. The Māori name for Avondale.

Whāwhāpō whāwhā (to feel about); pō (night). A young chief crawled into a camp and felt about with his hands at night.

Whāwhārua whāwhā (to feel about); rua (pit). To feel about in the store pit.

Whekenui wheke (octopus); nui (big). Te Wheke-a-muturangi is the name of the huge octopus that Kupe chased across Cook Strait and finally killed in Whekenui Bay.

Whenuahou *whenua* (land); *hou* (new). New country.

Whenuakite The full name, compressed by the Pākehā to Fenukit, is Te Whenua-i-kite-te-manu-aute-o-Tama-pahore, The land discovered by the paper-mulberry kite of Tama-pahore. This man flew a kite at Remuera. The string broke. The kite was followed until it came to earth at this place.

Whenuakura *whenua* (land); *kura* (red). The name was brought from Hawaiki by Turi of the Aotea canoe, and given in memory of the red feathers of a tropic bird.

Whenuanui *whenua* (country); *nui* (big). Plenty of land.

Whenuapai *whenua* (country); *pai* (good). Good land.

Whetūkura *whetū* (star); *kura* (red). Red star.

Whirinaki To lean, or the buttress of a house.

Whitianga The crossing, or the ford.

Wingatui Possibly the correct name is Whiringatua, the place of the plaiting of straps.

There is a story that comes from the founding of Otago. It is said that one of the settlers shot at and winged a tūī.

Wiri Named after Takaanini Wirihana, a Māori chief. Wirihana is Māori for Wilson. Literally, to shiver, or tremble.

Whitianga.

Appendix: European place names

The following European names are mentioned in the text. The Māori names which follow may be the original names, or may contain a reference to the European place name in the text. Some suburbs having Māori names are also listed under the cities.

Alum Creek Waimangeo
Anderson's Bay Puketai
Arrow River Haehaenui
  Kimiakau
Ashburton River Hakatere
Aspiring, Mount Tititea
Athens Ātene
Auckland Akarana
  Kahu, Kohimārama, Kōhuaora, Māngere,
  Manukau, Manurewa, Maungakiekie, Mokoia,
  Ōka, Onehunga, Otahuhu, Ōwairaka, Papakura,
  Papatoetoe, Pupuke, Rangitoto, Remuera,
  Takapuna, Tāmaki, Tauranga-mangō, Taurarua,
  Te Kūrae-o-tura, Te Pāpapa, Te Ranga-o-Taikehu,
  Te Tātua, Te Tō, Titirangi, Waiatarua, Waikomiti,
  Waitakere, Waitematā, Whau
Avon, River Ōrotore
  Ōtakaro, Ōtautahi
Avondale Whau

Balclutha Iwikatea
Bay of Islands Kahuwera
  Kerikeri, Kororāreka, Motu-arohia, Moturoa,
  Paihia, Peowhairangi, Taiamai, Tokerau
Bay View Pētane

Ben Ohou Aroaro-kaihe
Berea Peria
Bethany Pētane
Bethlehem Peterehāma
Bishop's Peninsula Huri-o-te-wai
Blenheim Waiharakeke
Bligh Sound Te Anahawea
Blue Lake Tikitapu
Bluff Motupiu
Boulder Bank Te Pokohiwi
Bowen Falls Hine-te-awa
Breaksea Sound Huihui-kōura
Brewster, Mount Haumaitikitiki
Brothers, The Ngā Whatu
Brunner, Lake Kōtuku
  Moana-kōtuku
Buller River Kawatiri
Burnett Range Kamautūrua

Cambridge Maungatautari
Camel, Mount Maungataniwha
Canaan Kenana
Canterbury Plains Ngā or Kā-pākihi-
  whakatekateka-a-Waitaha
Cargill, Mount Kapuka-tau-mohaka

Appendix: European place names

Cass Bay Motukauatiiti
Cass River Horokōau
Castlecliff Kai-hau-o-Kupe
Castle Rock Motutere
Christchurch Aranui
  Kaiapoi, Ōpawa, Ōrotore, Ōtakaro, Ōtautahi,
  Papanui, Pūtaringamotu
Clarence River Waiautoa
Clutha River Kāhuika
  Matau
Colville, Cape Moehau
  Te Kupenga-a-Taramainuku
Cook, Mount Aorangi
  Kirikiri-katata
Cook Strait Arahura
  Arapaoa, Ngā Whatu, Raukawa, Te Tao-o-Kupe
Corinth Koriniti
Coromandel Motutere
  Tapu, Whakatete
Corsair Bay Motukauatiiti
Croisilles Harbour Whangarae
Crown Range Haumaitikitiki
Curious Cove Kahikatea
Cyrene Hairini

Daggs Sound Te Rā
Damascus Ramaiku
Damper, Mount Aorangi
Dannevirke Umutaoroa
D'Archiac Kāhui-kau-peka
Devonport Te Kūrae-o-Tura
  Te Ranga-o-Taikehu
Dog Island Motupiu
Doubtful Sound Kāhui-kākāpo
Dunedin Kaikōrai
  Ōpoho, Ōtepoti, Puketai, Te Au,
  Te Ika-a-Paraheke, Wakāri
Dusky Sound Manutiti
  Motukiekie

East Cape Tapuwaeroa
Edwardson Arm Moanawhenuapōuri
Egmont/Taranaki, Mount Minarapa
  Tāhurangi, Tama-ahua, Taranaki

Ellesmere, Lake Kaikanohi
  Kaitorete, Ko-te-kete-ika-a-Tutekawa,
  Waihora
Eutychus Utiku

Fairy Springs Te Puna-a-Tūhoe
Farewell Spit Onetahua
Featherston Kaiwaiwai
Feilding Aorangi
Five Rivers Aparima
Flaxbourne Waiharakeke
Forsyth, Lake Ko-te-kete-ika-a-Tutekawa
  Wairewa
Foveaux Strait Ara-a-Kiwa
Freemans Bay Te Tō
French Pass Te Aumiti

Galatea Karatia
Galilee Kariri
Gisborne Mangapapa
  Tūranga, Waerenga-a-hika
Glen Eden Waikomiti
Goat Island Pūrakanui
Golgotha Korokata
Grassmere, Lake Kaipara-te-hau
Great Barrier Island Aotea
  Aotearoa
Great Mercury Island Ahuahu
Green Lake Rotokākahi
Greymouth Mawhera
Grey River Mawhera
  Moutapu
Greytown Houhou-pounamu
Grove Arm Iwirua

Haast Pass Tiori-pātea
Hall's Arm Kāhui-kākāpo
Hamilton Kirikiriroa
Hastings Heretaunga
Hawke Bay Te Matau-a-Māui
Hen and Chicken Islands Te Kupenga-a-
  Taramainuku
Holdsworth, Mount Taratahi
Howick Ōwairoa

Hutt Valley Epuni
  Heretaunga, Moerā, Naenae, Petone, Pōmare,
  Taitā, Te Ahi-a-manono, Waiwhetū

Invercargill Waikiwi

Jackson's Head Kupenga-a-Kupe
  Te Tao-o-Kupe
Jerusalem Hiruhārama
Judea Te Huria
Judge's Bay Taurarua

Kidnappers, Cape Tapuwaeroa
King Country Rohepōtae

Laodicea Raorikia
Lawyer's Head Te Ika-a-Parehika
Levin Horowhenua
Linton Te Kairanga
Little Barrier Island Hauturu
London Rānana
Lyall Bay Maranui
Lyttelton Okete-upoko
  Te Whakaraupō

Macedonia Makerōnia
Mackenzie country Aorangi
Marton Tūtaenui
Mayor Island Tūhua
McKerrow, Lake Wakatipuwaitai
McLaren's Peak Matapehi-o-te-rangi
Mercury Harbour Whanganui-o-Hei
Milford Sound Piopiotahi
  Te Pari
Moonlight Gully Ko-kohaka-ruru-whenua

Napier Ahuriri
  Hukarere, Keteketerau, Marewa, Pānia,
  Upoko-pōito
Nelson Horoirangi
  Koputīraha, Maitai, Tāhunanui, Wakapuaka,
  Wakatū
New Plymouth Ngāmotu
  Paritutū

Nile River Waitakere
Normanby Ketemarae
North Cape Muriwhenua
North Island Eaheinōmāuwe
  Nukuroa, Te Ika-a-Māui

One Tree Hill Maungakiekie

Pacific Ocean Moana-nui-a-Kiwa
Palliser, Cape Te Kawakawa
Palmerston North Awapuni
  Hokowhitu, Papaioea
Panmure Mokoia
Passage Island Motu-tawaki
Pelorus Sound Te Hoiere
Pepin Island Huri-o-te-wai
Philippi Piripai
Picton Waitohi
Port Chalmers Kopūtai
Port Levy Koukou-parata
Port Nicholson Pōneke
  Te Whanganui-a-Tara
Prospect, Mount Haumaitikitiki
Providence, Cape Kōurariki
Pumpkin Flat Te Pāpapa

Quail Island Ōtamahua
Queen Charlotte Sound Arapaoa
  Motuora

Raglan Harbour Whaingāroa
Rainbow Mountain Maungakaramea
Riccarton Pūtaringamotu
Riverton Pūkorokio
Russell Kororāreka
  Maiki

St John, Lake Waiatarua
Samaria Hamaria
Scinde Island Hukarere
Seatoun Tūranga
Sefton, Mount Aroaro-kaihe
Selwyn River Waikerikeri
Shag Point Ārai-te-uru

Appendix: European place names

Sheerdown, Mount Te Pari
Shelly Beach Ōkā
   Tauranga-mangō
Ship Cove Meretoto
Silberhorn, Mount Aorangi
Sinclair Head Rimurapa
Smyrna Hamurana
Somes Island Matiu
Southern Alps Kā-puke-māeroero
South Island Arahura
   Arapaoa, Kaikōura, Mahunui, Te Wai Pounamu
   Te Waka-a-Māui
Spey River Kāhui-kākāpo
Stevens Island Huihui-kōura
Stewart Island Rakiura
   Te Puka-a-Māui
Stop Island Motukiekie
Sumner, Lake Hakakura

Tasman, Mount Horokōau
Teichelmann, Mount Aorangi
Three Kings Te Tātua
Three Kings Island Manawa-tahi
Tom Bowling Bay Kapo-wairua

Torlesse, Mount Whataarama

Victoria, Mount Hātaitai

Warkworth Mahurangi
   Puhinui
Watchman, The Te Kupenga-a-Taramainuku
Weeks Island Puketutu
Wellington Hātaitai
   Karori, Makara, or Mākara, Maranui, Matairangi,
   Muritai, Ngaio, Ngāuranga, Ōhariu, Ōhiro,
   Ōtari, Rongotai, Te Aro, Te Kaminaru, Tinakori,
   Tūranga
Wellington Harbour Hātaitai
   Matiu, Pōneke, Te Whanganui-a-Tara
West Coast Poutini
   Te Ika-a-Māui
Whale Island Moturātā
White Island Whakaari
Wilto Ōtari

Young Nick's Head Te Kurī-a-Pawa

Zion Hiona